AUTOMOBILE AERODYNAMICS

AUTOMOBILE AERODYNAMICS

Theory and Practice for Road and Track

GEOFFREY HOWARD

OSPREY

Published in 1986 by Osprey Publishing Limited
27A Floral Street, London WC2E 9DP
Member company of the George Philip Group

Sole distributors for the USA

Motorbooks International
Publishers & Wholesalers Inc
Osceola, Wisconsin 54020, USA

British Library Cataloguing in Publication Data

Howard, Geoffrey
    Automobile aerodynamics: theory and practice
    for road and track.
    1. Automobiles—Aerodynamics
    I. Title
    629.2'31   TL245
ISBN 0-85045-665-7 ✓

Filmset by
Tameside Filmsetting Ltd, Ashton-under-Lyne, Lancashire
Printed by
BAS Printers Ltd, Over Wallop, Hampshire

Contents

Acknowledgements

I am deeply indebted to my one-time colleague on *Autocar*, Ted Eves, whose intimate knowledge of Formula 1 racing car design proved a great help with the chapter on Grand Prix aerodynamics; to Karl Ludvigsen for giving me access to his extensive historical archives; to Dr J. Harvey at my old college (Imperial, London) and to my many friends within the automotive industry for their cooperation, assistance and enthusiasm for the subject.

I am also grateful to the following for the provision of illustrations on the pages indicated:

Adam Opel AG (pages 78, 81 and 120), Aston Martin Lagonda (page 95), Aston Martin Tickford (page 105), Audi AG (pages 77, 91, 98, 108, 115 and 175), Austin Rover Group (pages 108, 173, 174 and 186), BL Technology (pages 88 and 181), Chrysler Corporation (pages 101 and 178), Citroen Cars (page 130), Daimler-Benz AG (pages 26 and 54), Daimler-Benz Museum Archives (pages 16, 19, 20 and 48), Edward Eves Archives (pages 139, 140, 141, 142, 143, 144, 145, 147, 150, 152, 154 and 156), Ford Motor Company (pages 11, 23, 24, 29, 34, 35, 61, 65, 66, 73, 74, 75, 76, 83, 86, 89, 90, 91, 93, 95, 97, 103, 104, 106, 111, 112, 113, 114, 115, 117, 118, 122, 132, 134, 135, 136, 159, 160, 163, 171, 172, 176, 183 and 184), General Motors Corporation (pages 68, 69, 100 and 187), Goodyear Tyre Company (page 84), Henry Ford Museum (page 58), Jaguar Cars (page 164), Motor Industry Research Association (pages 63 and 80), National Motor Museum (pages 10, 14, 39, 40, 42, 43, 44, 45, 47, 50, 51, 52 and 53), Nissan Motor Company (page 63), Peugeot Automobiles (page 128), Pininfarina Industrie SpA (page 33), Piper Cars (pages 163 and 165), Porsche Cars (pages 101, 102, 166, 167 and 169), Quadrant Autocar Archives (page 12), Regie Renault (page 129), Volkswagenwerk AG (pages 14, 16, 17, 22, 25, 28, 32, 36, 55, 62, 76, 79, 89, 93, 94, 97, 120, 126, 180 and 188).

Preface

Man has been intrigued by air flow since the beginning of his time on earth. Exactly when he first gained the intelligence to harness wind power, however crudely, cannot be far removed from the time he first learnt to relieve sliding friction by rollers and wheels, and to create fire for warmth and cooking.

It has taken nearly 5000 years of painfully slow technical evolution to progress from sails, windmills and kites to aeroplanes and motor cars. The obstacle to the progress so often dreamed of, but never achieved, was only removed in the nineteenth century, when materials and scientific theory took off to create the Industrial Revolution. Understanding, knowledge and expertise came with the means to build on sound engineering principles.

The science of managing air flow over man-made surfaces, like most modern technology, has advanced in a series of quantum leaps and bounds throughout this century. Nowhere is this more true than in aviation fields, where progress is best measured by the difference between the Wright brothers' first 12 second power-driven hop in 1903 and the Mach 2 Concorde which first entered commercial service in 1976. From a few precarious feet above the ground to a cruising altitude of 11 miles is an achievement just as remarkable as the boost from 30 mph to well over 1200 mph in speed.

The efficiency of shapes has been just as much a challenge to those working in the field of car design. Ever since the first self-propelled vehicles began to push the thresholds of speed up to the point where you could feel the airstream in your face, the search has been on to reduce drag by smoothing shapes in the most effective way. And the technology of aviation has repeatedly spilled over into the automotive arena.

The science of air behaviour in motion, described as aerodynamics, concerns the way in which air is disturbed by the movement of a solid body through it, and equally by the air flow over surfaces. This study of flow characteristics has developed far past the elementary need to measure the forces generated and energy dissipated. It has progressed into the complex interrelationships between every facet of vehicle performance, from drag forces, lift coefficients and yaw responses to cooling rates for engine and brakes, to heating and ventilation requirements for passenger comfort, to wiper effectiveness and window soiling in bad weather and to interior noise levels from the air flow itself. It has even affected the aesthetics of car shapes and the statement that their 'styling' attempts to make about the product it is packaging.

Aerodynamics, in spite of the highly developed computer age of this decade, is still essentially an empirical science. Only the simplest cases can be investigated mathematically and actual tests on wind tunnel models are the only way to predetermine what will be the final outcome of any design feature or detail change to a car's shape. In most instances, force measurements on three-dimensional scales provide engineering data that indicates the direction of development. Sometimes visualization of flow patterns can be helpful too, to illustrate the precise point of flow separation or the exact nature of energy-wasting turbulence.

This 'black art' element in the process of body design, combined with the historical roots of shape responsibility lying firmly in the car stylist's camp, has led to widespread ignorance of aerodynamic design on a considerable scale. This book has been written to explain the very involved business of aerodynamics in car design. It describes the historical influences on today's practices, the achievements from the past and the trends for the future. It looks at the engineers' work tools, their methods and their progress—for production cars intended for road use and for racing cars that provide so much track spectacle. It is both a text book and an enthusiast's guide, where hopefully even the expert can find something he didn't know before.

Geoffrey Howard
Halstead
June 1986

1 First attempts to streamline

Ever since man started to travel at more than a walking pace, he appreciated the strength of wind resistance. This wind tunnel test on a racing cyclist conducted by Volkswagen shows how both the frontal area and the drag coefficient can be reduced by crouching over the handlebars

Even the early cyclists of the nineteenth century knew that the faster they pedalled the greater the air resistance on their faces and bodies. When cycles became motorized, the riders also learned that by crouching low over the handlebars they could improve the performance of the engine, to climb hills better or gain more speed. But it took Camille Jenatzy's 1899 world land speed record of over 100 km/h (62 mph) in *La Jamais Contente* to turn the spotlight on the potential benefits which aerodynamics had to offer.

At that time, despite all the efforts of such visionaries as the 'father' of aviation, Leonardo da Vinci, and even the famous first recorded free flight in a simple hang-glider by Eilmer, the mad monk of Malmesbury, around AD 1000, there was widespread ignorance of the science needed to design shapes where the air flow could be controlled as it passed over the surface of the structure. Sir George Cayley's work on a model glider in 1804, followed by Otto Lilienthal's studies of

Camille Jenatzy was the first land speed record breaker to realize the importance of streamlining when he took his torpedo-shaped electric car (La Jamais-Contente) to over 100 km/h (62 mph) in 1899. He failed to appreciate how much drag his own body was creating, however

bird mechanics 50 years later, went a long way to advancing the art which later led to Wilbur and Orville Wright successfully adding a power unit to their glider in 1903. This flight, incidentally, came only after their engine and propeller had been used to drive one of the first known wind tunnels, which they built for control surface tests in 1902.

But as well as the winged-aviation pioneers there had been considerable progress in refining the shapes of marine hulls and also intense efforts to develop commercially viable airship transport. Each had its own influence on car design, from the 'torpedo' shell used by Jenatzy to the work of the Lebaudy brothers and Count Ferdinand von Zeppelin on the aerodynamics of airships.

In the early 1900s there were many and various attempts to streamline certain features of racing cars, with only moderate effectiveness and mostly without regard

RIGHT *The 1902 Ford Model N was a typical example of how the early designers made their first token gestures to aerodynamics with a toeboard fairing designed to deflect the air smoothly over the occupants above and through the radiator below*

for the *total* air flow pattern. In 1902 Baron de Rothschild's racing Mercedes appeared with an enveloping nose-scuttle cowl, the same year that Baker built a streamlined electric racer with a claimed top speed of more than 85 mph, well in excess of the world land speed record officially recognized in Europe. In 1904 the Baker Electric Torpedo attained 104 mph on the 23-mile long Ormond-Daytona Beach, Florida, but only in one direction and was therefore not officially recognized by the European motor sport commission in Paris.

The Baker Electric Racer weighed about 3100 lb because of its battery load, but was advanced in every other respect. It had a long wheelbase and low centre of gravity for stability at speed, considerable strength in its structure and a classic teardrop outline between exposed wheels with full disc covers on both sides, features that did not appear again on record breakers until 1927. Driver and riding mechanic sat in tandem beneath a slim covered cockpit, ahead of the motor and surrounded by lead-acid batteries.

The Autocar of 31 January 1903 described the body structure in detail:

Baker's conception of the body form of his racer also reverts to marine types. The underframe of the waggon takes the form of a shallow flat-bottomed barge, somewhat narrowed at each end, suspended beneath the axles. The upper body closely follows yacht-hull lines, and the whole vehicle is really a decked yacht-hull turned bottom side up, so that the deck forms the bottom of the carriage body, smooth and free from all projections, while a very small and low hatch coaming, provided with a curved mica

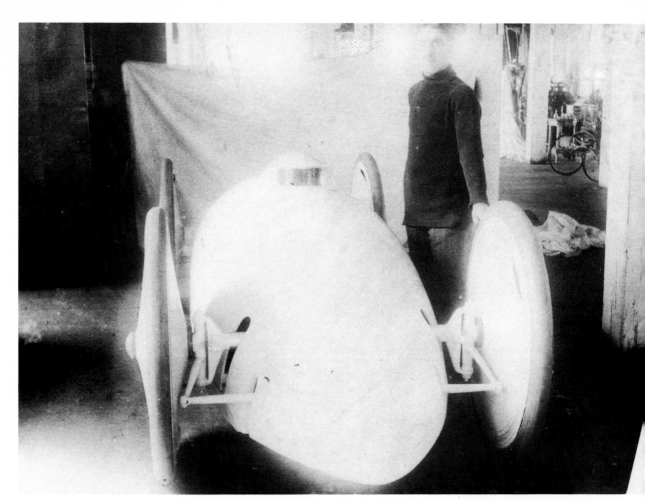

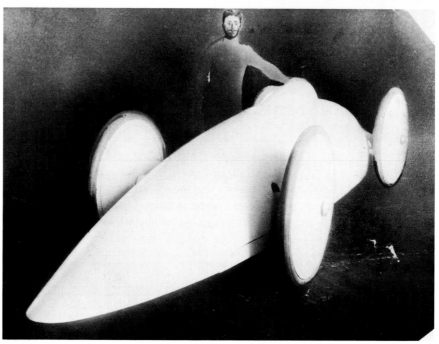

window, rises from the upturned keel to contain the driver's head, and permit him to have an unobstructed view of the sides and front of his road.

To avoid air resistance and the catching up and throwing of pebbles and road drift, the wheel spokes are covered with white enamelled cloth, which is whole on the outsides of the wheels, except for a hole for the hub end, and is carried over the wheel rim, under the pneumatic tyres, and then turns down the inside of the wheel for a couple of inches or so, leaving the insides of the wheels to be covered by other pieces of the same white enamelled cloth, which are laced at their outer edges to the outer cover.

Some other early designers were obviously sufficiently aware of basic air flow principles to devote time and trouble to reducing turbulence in the wake of their high, square-backed vehicles. An article describing studies of the air flow behind fast cars was published in *Omnia, Revue Practique de Locomotion*, in 1909, based on the work of one W.R. Cooper who devised some ingenious ways of measuring both the direction and pressure of turbulence at the condenser intake, behind the front wheels and in the slipstream of a 1903 White steam car. A bamboo pole 10 feet long was extended behind the vehicle and fitted with a string and pulley system to transmit the forces on small flaps to a car-mounted needle gauge.

Probably one of the most advanced attempts to control air flow came in 1909, when a certain Mr W. Heap Holland commissioned English coachbuilders Max Graddon & Lawson Ltd to construct a special body on a 20–30 hp Austro-Daimler. Holland had developed a theory far ahead of his time that the broad square back of the conventional open tourer contributed more than the front surfaces to the total wind resistance.

Unaware that some 70 years later this area of car shapes was to prove critical in the development of low drag bodies, he tried to reduce the underbody turbulence and control the energy-absorbing eddy currents created in the wake behind the car. His special body featured a venturi air tunnel through the rear of the car and carefully moulded smooth rear panels. There is no record of how effective the device proved to be, but there could hardly have been any means of measuring it at that time.

By 1913 Count Ricotti had achieved over 136.9 km/h (85 mph) on the road from Milan to Como in his Alfa with the amazing teardrop-shaped Castagna body that could easily have returned a drag coefficient of below 0.3, were it not for some of the fittings and the very inefficient aerodynamics of the underbody area. But the greatest pioneer of aerodynamic technology was undoubtedly Paul Jaray, an Austrian-born engineer who in 1910 graduated from the German Technical College of Prague.

After a brief period designing aircraft for Count von Zeppelin, he began aerodynamic studies on airships and was instrumental in commissioning one of the first scientific wind tunnels in 1916. After World War 1 in 1921, he turned his attention to car design, testing many wooden models in the Zeppelin tunnel. Although this was the largest in Germany, with a diameter of nearly 10 feet, Jaray already knew enough about aerodynamic science and testing to realize that the walls would interfere with the flow over a full-size car, so he used only 1:10 scale models.

To determine total drag, he suspended each model on its side by wires and measured the force required to keep it from moving, correcting the result for the effect of the wires and their attachments. He developed a proposed low drag shape from these tests for which he claimed, in an article published in 1922, a coefficient of only 0.28 at a time when the established state of the art was producing car bodies

By 1903 the state of the aerodynamic art had advanced tremendously in some quarters, but severely lagged in others. The Baker Electric Torpedo, which achieved 104 mph on a Florida beach the following year, was several decades ahead of its time with a teardrop profile, a fully enclosed underbody and elaborate laced wheel covers

ABOVE *It was almost ten years before another car appeared with such advanced aerodynamic features as the Baker Electric Torpedo. This is the Castagna-bodied Alfa Romeo 40/60 which achieved over 136 km/h (85 mph) on the public road from Milan to Como in 1913 with a full-sized limousine shell utilizing curved glass for the first time*

RIGHT *Paul Jaray, like Dr Edmund Rumpler, produced some exceptionally low drag body designs. The only one ever to reach production was this rear-engined 1934 Tatra V8, made in Czechoslovakia with a drag coefficient of 0.36*

around 0.7. In 1939 the same model was retested by Daimler-Benz in their Stuttgart tunnel, which produced a value of 0.245.

The Jaray secret was to consider the complete car as a total package, for he was well aware that any changes made to one part of the body created an interrelated effect on the others. In this appreciation of the fundamentals of air flow management he was probably almost alone at that time, most other attempts at drag reduction being performed on a piecemeal basis with very little tunnel testing.

Many patents were filed by Jaray on the subject of aerodynamics in the following years and they included interesting innovations. In 1923 he was the first designer after Baker to close in the cockpit of a racing car—a technique which brought many victories and plenty of copies—and he developed the first effective means of ventilating closed cars without draughts, again by careful air flow management. He even managed to duct engine heat to the passengers, controlling its effect by the degree of window opening, and arranged for rain to be swept off his curved windscreens by air flow techniques.

Commercially, the brilliance of Paul Jaray never paid off, although he designed aerodynamic cars in abundance, including special bodies for a 2-litre Mercedes and a 2-litre Audi in 1934, followed by a 3.8-litre Maybach. The only product to appear in quantity production with his unmistakeable touch was the distinctive rear-engined 1934 Tatra V8 made in Czechoslovakia (measured in the Volkswagen wind tunnel in 1982 with a drag coefficient of 0.36). He was simply ahead of his time, born in the wrong era and dedicated to techniques which had little place or need in a society more interested in fashion, style and the visible display of opulence.

What he actually contributed to car design was research and insight into the development of shapes and ways to improve their efficiency of movement. He also went further into the science we now know as air flow management, or ways of controlling and using the pressures generated on the surface of a body. While he did not have the means to measure all the variables possible today, he was certainly well aware of the potential value of what he was doing.

Even before Jaray, aircraft influences were filtering through to car design, and a truly remarkable example of this was the 1921 Rumpler. Unlike the slim-bodied racing cars and record breakers purpose-built to reach extraordinary high speeds for their day, the Rumpler was a full-sized four-seater saloon. In 1983 it was tested in the Volkswagen wind tunnel and returned an amazing drag coefficient of only 0.28.

Although Dr Edmund Rumpler started his career in the early days of Adler, he switched to aircraft design and only returned to the car industry in 1918. By applying aircraft principles to body design, he developed his famous 'teardrop' shape (long established as the most efficient aerodynamic form for movement through air, see Chapter 2) powered by a rear-mounted 2.6-litre 6-cylinder engine mounted in the rear ahead of the axle. Its debut at the 1921 Berlin Motor Show was little short of a sensation.

One of Rumpler's associates and fellow aviators, Hellmuth Hirth, went to work for Benz in Germany in 1913 and was so impressed with Rumpler's aerodynamics that he persuaded Benz to take up the design. An open Rumpler 'Tropfen-Auto' (the German name for a teardrop shape) was therefore shipped to the Benz factory in 1921 as the starting point in a new aerodynamic passenger car development programme. And to gain publicity for the new concepts involved, a Benz 'Tropfenwagen' racing car was designed for the 1922 Grand Prix season. The bodywork of the first Benz Tropfenwagen, built as a prototype only, in 1922,

ABOVE *Rumpler's earlier work inspired this Benz Tropfenwagen racing car built for the 1922 Grand Prix season using a full teardrop profile and an extremely low driving position. It was further developed with the addition of 'wings'*

RIGHT *The amazing 1921 boat-shaped Rumpler used aircraft principles to demonstrate how a teardrop planform could be used to provide low drag with roomy accommodation for four people. The Rumpler was tested in the VW wind tunnel in 1983 and recorded a drag coefficient of only 0.28*

followed the classic teardrop shape which in its purest wheel-less form can achieve drag coefficient as low as 0.10. Its profile and cross-section were actually close to those of the 1904 Baker Electric Torpedo, but with a more rounded nose and open-spoked wheels. It was slim, elegant and extremely efficient.

Some of its features played an important role in the achievement of low drag. It was crab-tracked (6 in. less at the rear than the front), to pull the air flow in towards the pointed tail and reduce the size of the energy-wasting wake. And the aircraft-type radiator was mounted on top of the body behind the mid engine with a beautiful polished brass header tank that reproduced the teardrop shape in miniature.

Three of these cars, modified during development to meet the practical requirements of racing, first appeared in the 1923 European Grand Prix at Monza. Two of them finished honourably, in fourth and fifth places, winning a special award for the most outstanding new cars in the race. But the inflationary troubles of the German economy soon brought the Benz company into partnership with Daimler, curtailing the competition programme and work on aerodynamic cars. One Tropfenwagen was converted into a sports car with headlamps and wing-shaped mudguards, performing well in sprints and hillclimbs in 1924 and 1925.

The emphasis this teardrop technology brought to 'streamlining' (an ill-conceived descriptive term which has since fallen into disrepute) introduced a rash of special aerodynamic bodies to the racing car and record breaking world of the decadent twenties and thirties. The 1926 French Gerin, with its light alloy body and

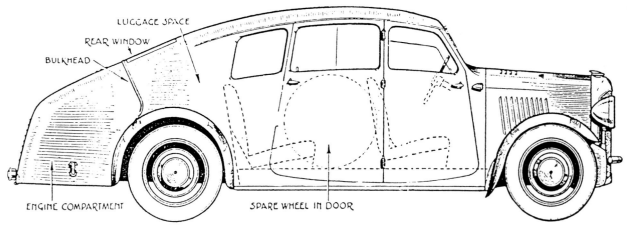

LUGGAGE SPACE

REAR WINDOW

BULKHEAD

ENGINE COMPARTMENT

SPARE WHEEL IN DOOR

fuselage section, and the 1927 Claveau both followed Rumpler's formula with engines behind the cabin and long pointed tails.

Another aircraft manufacturer transferring techniques into car production was Gabriel Voisin, a man dedicated to all manner of advanced ideals including low vehicle weight and minimum aerodynamic drag. His wood and aluminium bodies were incredibly ugly and never sold at all well.

Airship designer Sir Dennistoun Burney also used aircraft construction for his 1928 *Streamline* prototype, shaped on the teardrop principle and based on a front-drive Alvis chassis turned back to front. Only 12 were ever made, the 1930s depression killing it off along with most other original but expensive concepts.

But out of the ill-fated Benz Tropfenwagen came the mid-engined Auto Union Type C in 1934, a practical rationalization of the ideal teardrop for the 750 kg Grand Prix weight limit. It was the brainchild of Dr Ferdinand Porsche and achieved more than 322 km/h (200 mph) from only 280 bhp. In 1937, with the supercharged engine enlarged to 6.3 litres and developing over 520 bhp, it went on first to 402.5 km/h (250 mph) and then with further aerodynamic improvements to 442 km/h (275 mph).

The mid-1930s were dominated in Nazi Germany at least by a keen spirit of competition in what really amounted to a technology race between Auto Union and Mercedes-Benz. Almost overnight, speed record breaking became a national pastime in a field which historically had always been left to the British, the French, the Italians and even the Americans. Typical of the German way, it was not done by brute force and aerodynamic ignorance but by scientific development that extended to some extreme lengths. And its purpose was not so much to make technological progress as to demonstrate the world supremacy of Hitler's 'master race'. . . .

The venue for many speed records and speed attempts was the high-speed banked Avus circuit near Berlin, first opened in 1921 and rebuilt in 1937 specially for high speed. But because its gradient of 3 per cent prohibited official ratification of any achievements, the wonderful new concrete *autobahns* were the scene of many high speed runs.

It was the building of special cars for this task that led to most of the pre-World War 2 advancement in aerodynamic knowledge and techniques. Using redundant Grand Prix chassis and highly-developed supercharged engines (up to 700 bhp from a 5-litre V12), Mercedes-Benz went after the Class B (engines from 5 to 8 litres) speed record with a car that set totally new aerodynamic standards. Working in the Zeppelin wind tunnel at Friedrichshafen a new streamlined body was developed

LEFT *In 1928 the famous airship designer, Sir Dennistoun Burney, produced another teardrop prototype which he called the* Streamline. *It appeared at several motor shows but only a handful were ever built*

BELOW *Lessons learned with the Benz Tropfenwagen were later applied to the 1934 Auto Union Type C Grand Prix car, the brainchild of Dr Ferdinand Porsche. In 1937 it took a speed record at over 442 km/h (275 mph)*

The late 1930s saw plenty of high-speed record breaking, much of it on Hitler's marvellous new concrete autobahns *that were being built right across Germany. In 1936 Mercedes-Benz developed their supercharged V12 Grand Prix engine to* produce more than 700 bhp, installed it in a low drag body and reached more than 367 km/h (228 mph) between Frankfurt and Darmstadt

during 1936 that recorded a drag coefficient of only 0.232 using a fully enclosed underpan and ducted radiator cooling. There were lift problems (see Chapter 11), solved by the addition of lead ballast, but this car with covered front wheels eventually achieved 367 km/h (228 mph) on the Frankfurt–Darmstadt *autobahn*.

The next year the same basic shape was narrowed by nearly 9 in. and lowered by about 4 in. to reduce its frontal area by more than 10 per cent. Lengthening the body by 16 in. helped cut the Cd to only 0.181. Closing off the radiator intake and using ice in a closed-circuit cooling system (sufficient for a single high-speed run), reduced the Cd to only 0.157, measured from 52 drag readings on a full-size car in the Berlin wind tunnel of the German Aviation Research Establishment. There were small openings in the nose to supply the engine with air (it breathed more than 500 litres/sec. at maximum speed), but a record average of over 268 mph was duly achieved over a measured mile in two directions.

Between 1937 and 1939, aerodynamic research continued, producing an interesting new shape development from Professor W.I.E. Kamm of the Stuttgart Technical High School. He designed a body, called the K-car, with what he described as 'the smallest interrupted cross-section'. Kamm's studies into air flow patterns exposed the folly of the long teardrop tail, which failed to maintain smooth laminar flow and only served to introduce excessive friction drag. His solution was to cut the bodywork off sharply at the point where the optimum flow separated, providing the smallest interrupted cross-section for the drag inducing wake behind the vehicle which inevitably is highly turbulent. His Kamm-backed saloon recorded a drag coefficient of 0.37 in recent tests.

It was Kamm's asserted claim that production cars of the late 1930s operated with a fuel consumption 25 per cent higher than was technically attainable at that time. He believed that aerodynamic drag could be reduced by between 28 to 45 per cent with relative ease, a fact demonstrated by researchers in the twenties. Yet the car industry consistently turned its back on the advantages that were there simply for the taking.

There were many reasons why the car repeatedly missed out in the efficient development of its shape. Unlike boats, aeroplanes and even trains, which featured smooth, sleek designs consuming the least possible energy in their movement, the car stayed predominently square, upright and really very rough round the edges. It took both an energy crisis and a rapid rise in fuel prices for public acceptance of aerodynamic shapes to become a reality and even a marketing feature.

At the root of the sluggishness of car shape evolution is the consumer and function orientation of car design. Cars are high capital value goods, frequently changing hands in a buoyant, high-profit market that is only now starting to reach saturation in some Western countries, after 100 years of growth. Primarily, cars are people carriers, at least for the bulk of the 300 million people in the world today who run one. They are normally second in value only to a house in each of our lives, yet in Europe alone about 100 cars leave factory production lines every minute of every working shift.

When most of the world's oil supply came from the USA, which also made the most cars, there was little incentive to reduce the fuel they used. But the development of Middle East oil fields changed the balance of world economics after World War 2 (see Chapter 8) and industrial growth reduced the car from the world's largest user of energy to a position where, in Europe today, less than a quarter of the oil consumed is used in motor vehicles and only half of that in cars.

The mechanics of vehicle motion have been well understood for many years, but

Between 1937 and 1939 Professor Kamm developed a new low drag theory using a sharply cut off tail to generate a 'virtual' teardrop without the cumbersome weight and length. When tested recently this saloon recorded a drag coefficient of 0.37

for far too long car stylists and car engineers worked in conflict, not harmony. The artistic background to car styling created a gulf with the 'nuts and bolts' of the working parts, encouraged in the early days by the construction actually being undertaken separately as a running chassis to which the coachwork was later added.

With unitary construction, first applied to steel bodies in the 1930s, came a closer working relationship between the two factions which eventually merged into what is often referred to today as 'design engineering'. Within that field is where the car aerodynamicist is usually found, working on a science that involves every aspect of the air flow pattern round a car. This includes drag and lift forces, cross-wind stability, cooling flow rates, heater and ventilation performance, window soiling, wind noise and every other climatic effect likely to affect the vehicle and its occupants.

Lately, aerodynamic science has turned into a kind of technology race between manufacturers competing even harder for the same car buyers. Contrary to the popularly held misconception, it is proven fact that aerodynamic forces generate energy-significant effects from speeds as low as 35 mph. And the techniques required to reduce these values are evolving from a black art into a valuable commercial asset.

2 Mechanics of air flow

Total resistive forces on a car are the sum of the mechanical losses and the air drag. Mechanical losses are caused by the friction and rotational inertia of the drive train and tyres; air drag is caused by the resistance of the shape to the molecules of air which must be moved aside for it to pass. Mechanical losses go up in proportion to speed, while air drag rises more steeply according to a squared relationship. At about 40 mph on a modern European car, air drag becomes the larger force and by 70 mph it is several times the value of the mechanical drag. On American cars, which generally tend to be larger in scale and less efficient aerodynamically, air drag becomes the larger force at even lower speeds.

Form drag

There are basically five different causes of aerodynamic drag on a car, each of which makes a significant contribution to the total. The primary and most important factor is the *form drag*. This is the resistance caused by the basic shape, derived from its proportions and its size. It is the energy required to push the air molecules apart as it moves, so it is influenced by both the distance each molecule moves and the angle at which it is deflected.

In the simplest and idealized case, consider a car as a purely physical body

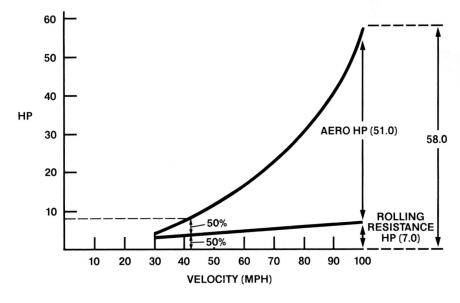

While the rolling resistance to motion rises in proportion to the speed, the air drag follows a square law and the aerodynamic horsepower absorbs power according to a cube relationship as these curves for the Ford Escort show. From about 42 mph, aerodynamic drag is the larger of the two

moving through the air, without the complications of turbulence, rotating wheels and internal air flow. As it moves it deflects each molecule at each point of its surface more or less through the same path. That path, which can be visualized by adding markers like smoke to the air flow, is known as a streamline.

The maximum distance the streamlines are stretched apart (they are parallel in a steady, stabilized and undisturbed air flow) is determined by the largest transverse section of the body—the silhouette (sometimes known as the 'flat plate' area) or the projected frontal area. Strictly speaking, and also a commonly held misconception, 'frontal area' is the cross-sectional area at the most forward vertical part of the car, usually at the entry point to the radiator. But in aerodynamic circles, convention defines frontal area as the full area of the vehicle at a theoretical visual infinity as seen from in front or behind.

Different shapes with the same frontal area can generate very different drag forces because air molecules absorb different amounts of energy depending on how violently they are deflected, for reasons which will be explained later in this chapter. The addition of a 60 degree nose cone, for example, cuts the drag on a flat plate by around 50 per cent, while a more pointed 30 degree nose cone cuts it by some 70 per cent. And a teardrop, which actually parts the streamlines totally without flow separation or surface turbulence (a phenomenon known as 'laminar flow' conditions), generates about four or five times less drag than a simple flat-based cone, point-on to the air stream.

But a shape like a car body is not smooth or simple and the pressure variations set up by its movement can easily cause the flow to separate from the surface in any number of localized and highly turbulent eddies, especially if an edge or some sharply changing radius introduces disturbances to the flow pattern. By the simple law of energy conservation, the energy absorbed by each of these eddies on its own as the molecules swirl about must all be added to the total drag. In effect, localized turbulences of this type give the shape a 'ragged' surface which, although only rough in a virtual way, is just as inefficient as a physically rough finish.

The flow pattern around a car body can be predetermined fairly accurately, in terms of where localized eddies will be generated, where there will be stagnant air, and so on. For studying flow patterns around the hulls of boats, models are towed on a carriage through a long tank of water and in the early days of automotive aerodynamics, flow patterns were often visualized by placing scale half models on

RIGHT *In its simplest form, a car body moving through the air parts the molecules and absorbs energy according to its physical size and its shape. The difference between the basic block (above) and the more realistic model (below) can be seen by the relative deflection of the streamlines, visualized by smoke trails*

BELOW *The aerodynamic component of vehicle drag forces is the net result of positive pressures acting on the forward facing surfaces and negative pressures on the rearward side. The more these forces are balanced, the lower the total drag produced*

TWO COMPONENTS
1. AERODYNAMIC DRAG "D"
2. ROLLING RESISTANCE "R"

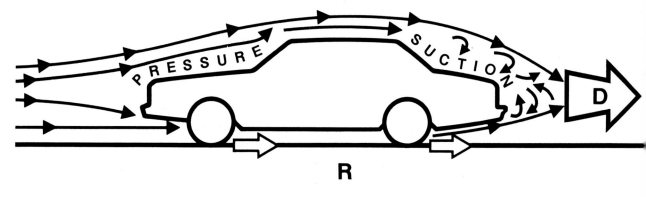

Smoke-emitting nozzles are frequently used in wind tunnels to show the air flow pattern over the surface of a car, to identify where there are turbulent eddies caused by flow separation. The smoother the air flow, the lower the drag

In addition to smoke-emitting nozzles, hundreds of individually applied wool tufts are also used to show the direction of the air flow at any point on the body surface and where there is unwanted turbulence

their side in a water tank and using dye tracers, like potassium permanganate, to identify the streamlines.

Later, flexible wool tufts were fixed to the body surface and the car photographed at various air speeds either on the road or in the wind tunnel to determine turbulent areas. Smoke nozzles, usually discharging a fine oil mist, are more often used now in the wind tunnel, as are streams of helium-filled weightless soap bubbles.

To measure flow direction accurately, a device taken from the aeronautical industry known as a *Flug Log* is often used. This is a flight test instrument mounted on a freely-floating body attached to a thin-section articulated support arm (called a 'sting' from its similarity to an insect's protective mechanism). The *Flug Log* aligns itself with the air flow direction and produces voltage outputs proportional to the angular displacement, relative to the sting. Small pinwheel rotors are also used to determine the direction of eddy turbulences and provide through their rotational speed a measure of the energy being absorbed.

This device, known as a Flug Log, is also used to measure the energy absorbed by eddies. It aligns itself with the air flow direction and spins at a speed proportional to the local air velocity, generating a voltage signal

Surface drag

Although air is made up of gases with very little viscosity, or resistance to the rate at which they change shape, it is far from being free from viscous effects under pressure. The kinematic viscosity of air is about one thirteenth that of water and it causes another kind of aerodynamic resistance known as *surface drag*. It is a kind of skin friction which increases the more the area is exposed to the air stream. Adding length to the centre of a car, and changing nothing else, will therefore increase its surface drag and thus the total resistive forces to motion.

When there is a differential speed between layers in any fluid, it shears like a sliding pack of cards. As a car body moves through the air its surface creates this shearing effect, with the velocity of each layer varying according to its distance from the surface. As the air molecules escape from each faster moving layer to a slower moving layer, there is a transfer of momentum which absorbs energy, converting it to heat. At supersonic speeds it is precisely this skin friction that raises the temperature of Concorde's exterior surface by more than 60 degrees Celsius, causing the length of the aircraft to expand by as much as 7 in. at Mach 2.

The distance between the body surface and the nearest point of undisturbed flow is known as the *boundary layer* thickness. And the variation in speed across the layer, known as its velocity gradient, depends upon the amount of surface friction. In extreme conditions, a high velocity gradient across the boundary layer can cause further surface eddies which absorb energy. If the velocity gradient is low, the flow remains smooth and laminar.

Induced drag

Asymmetric shapes moving through the air produce asymmetric pressures and therefore vertically acting forces, which in production cars usually act upwards as lift. The generation of these forces requires energy that increases total aerodynamic drag by what is known as the *lift-induced drag*. Another analysis explains lift-induced drag as the horizontal component of the lift generated, which is never purely vertical.

Lift forces in a moving vehicle are usually a function of the basic shape, which is not unlike a crude aircraft wing in profile. Lift in aircraft wings is generated by the difference in air velocity over the upper and lower surfaces, which causes a pressure differential. Similar differences exist in a car body, although various techniques and devices can be used to reduce lift and even generate downforce (see Chapters 10 and 11). Induced drag is also caused by the generation of downforce as this too is never purely vertical.

As the air flow accelerates over the upper surface of a car body (it has a greater distance to travel than the air passing underneath), it reduces in pressure. There is therefore a greater net pressure below the car than above it, which results in lift forces on front and rear axles. The magnitude of the lift is not normally sufficient to give the driver any cause for concern at speeds below 60 mph. At higher speeds it can reduce the steering effort required by lightening the reaction through the tyres from the road and crosswinds can deflect the car off course or set up disturbing instabilities (see Chapter 5).

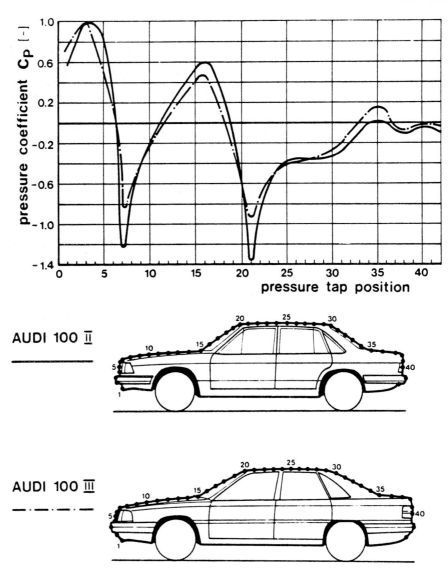

There are considerable variations in surface pressure across a car body, as these comparisons between two versions of the Audi 100 show very clearly. The difference between the net pressure on the upper and lower surfaces generates lift and drag

Interference drag

Adding body fittings and projections to a basically smooth exterior shape introduces what is known as *interference drag*. All items like number plates, windscreen wipers, door mirrors, headlamp rims, trim strips, window mouldings, radio aerial, door handles, bumper over-riders and spot lamps interfere with the smooth air flow to generate energy absorbing eddies and turbulences. Opening a side window or sunroof, adding a roof-rack or even a towing attachment all add significantly to the drag forces generated.

Under the floor of the car interference drag is caused by the exhaust system, suspension members, engine sump, spare wheel (when mounted under the boot floor), fuel tank and even small features like cross members and jacking points. Significant drag reductions can therefore be achieved by developing smoother belly pans and recessing as many components as possible out of the air flow. Care must be taken, however, to protect the functional requirements of cooling and service accessibility.

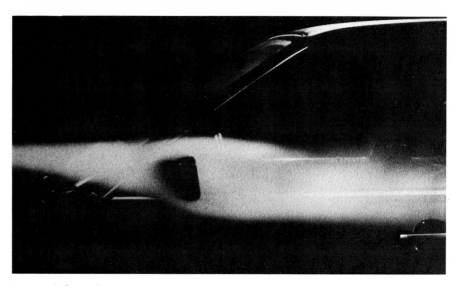

Any item that interrupts the air flow, like this door mirror, generates additional aerodynamic resistance known as interference drag. There are many other body features which act on the air flow in the same way

Internal flow drag

As well as passing over, under and around a car, air is also required to feed and cool the engine, to cool the brakes and to provide heating and ventilation for the occupants. These air flows generate *internal flow drag*. Design of intake and outlet areas for these functions is fundamental to the operation of the vehicle and one of the key items in the development of new model programmes.

In pure aerodynamic studies these vital elements are often overlooked in spite of the fact that they easily contribute more than 10 per cent of the total drag resistance. Very often there is little that can be done to reduce the values of internal flow drag after the mechanical configuration of the various sytems has been fixed. Before that stage the options are much greater.

To show how much effect interference drag and internal flow drag can deteriorate an otherwise efficient aerodynamic shape, it is interesting to study the famous Pininfarina 'Banana' car first shown publicly in 1978. Working on an ideal mathematical form developed over two years by Professor Alberto Morelli of the Turin Polytechnic College, Pininfarina built a full-size model that recorded a wind tunnel drag coefficient between 0.16 and 0.17, about one third of the average value for production cars at that time.

By adding the functional requirements of an engine colling system, door mirrors and windscreen wipers, the drag coefficient increased to 0.23. With sheet metal panels, openings for doors, bonnet and boot, plus provision of real glass in the windows, flush bonded to eliminate ridges, even this theoretically 'perfect' shape would probably be no better than an advanced production car like the Audi 100 or Renault 25.

New generations of advanced car shapes are now being designed to cut down internal flow drag as much as possible, by optimized below-bumper radiator intakes, ducted cooling air passages and the use of low-pressure fan-boosted heater inlets. Some experimental design studies, like the Ford Probe IV, have also appeared with a more innovative approach that repositions the radiator in the rear (see Chapter 9), for this reason entirely. In striving for new high speed records in the 1920s and 1930s, several designers closed off the radiator intake completely and cooled the engine for the few minutes required with ice.

Eventually it should be possible to utilize waste engine heat to eliminate internal flow drag completely, by efficient application of basic thermodynamics to convert heat to work, although no attempts have been made in this direction yet. Using engine power to dissipate waste heat with the aid of a cooling fan is contrary to the first law of energy efficiency and something which is bound to receive attention before long. An experimental proposal not yet proven employs a device called the Sodium Heat Engine that can convert heat directly into electrical energy.

Air flow physics: units, measures and coefficients

Fluids are substances which can flow in a readily distortable way. They have no shape of their own. Solids react to forces by generating internal shear stresses that distort them in proportion to the load up to the point at which they start to yield. Fluids, in contrast, have an internal resistance to the *rate* of change, not to the change of shape itself. When at rest, fluids have no internal shear stress.

Liquids and gases are all categorized as fluids. Liquids offer a much greater resistance to change of volume than gases, which are relatively easy to compress or

Pininfarina's 'Banana' car, first revealed in 1978, was developed over two years in the Turin Polytechnic to record a drag coefficient of less than 0.17. Adding engine cooling, door mirrors and windscreen wipers increased this to 0.23

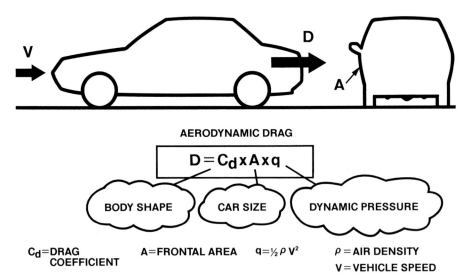

AERODYNAMIC DRAG

$$D = C_d \times A \times q$$

BODY SHAPE   CAR SIZE   DYNAMIC PRESSURE

C_d = DRAG COEFFICIENT   A = FRONTAL AREA $q = \frac{1}{2}\rho V^2$ ρ = AIR DENSITY

V = VEHICLE SPEED

The total resistive drag force (given the symbol D or F) is the product of the drag coefficient (Cd), the frontal area (A) and the dynamic air pressure (q)

expand to fit their containing vessel. Liquids in general have a density about a thousand times that of gases. Atmospheric air, of course, is a mixture of gases, being about 78 to 80 per cent nitrogen and 20 per cent oxygen. It behaves dynamically like any other gas.

As energy cannot be created or destroyed (it can only be converted from one form to another, usually from heat to work or vice-versa), the physics of air flow movement is governed by quite a simple law, known as Bernoulli's Theorem. It states that along any one streamline in a moving fluid, the total energy per unit mass is constant and equal to the sum of the potential energy, the pressure energy and the kinetic energy.

At the same temperature therefore, static and dynamic air pressure must always add up to the same constant value. Dynamic air pressure is equal to the air mass density times half the air speed squared.

Written in symbolic form, if p = static pressure and q = dynamic pressure:

$$p + q = k \text{ (a constant) and } q = \frac{\rho \times v^2}{2}$$

Where ρ is the air mass density and v the air stream speed.

When all the total pressures over the surface of a car in a moving stream of air are added together, the resultant dynamic pressure vector can be converted into a series of components which for convenience are considered as acting in three conventional planes (X, Y and Z axes). These components act as forces and as couples, which are usually called the turning moments (a 'couple' or 'moment' of a force about a given point is its turning effect, measured as the product of the force times the perpendicular distance between its line of action and the point in question).

The total horizontal force caused by the atmosphere opposing movement of the car is the aerodynamic resistive force (F), or the total vehicle drag force. It is proportional to the dynamic air pressure (hence the air speed squared), the area of the largest cross-section (frontal area or flat plate area) and a dimensionless coefficient of drag, usually given the symbol Cd (Cw in Germany, Cx in France).

There is no easy way to calculate drag coefficient and even attempts at computer modelling are taking a long time to reach sensible levels of prediction accuracy. Drag coefficients can only be determined accurately from empirical drag force measurements made in a calibrated wind tunnel.

As F = Cd × A × q, the drag coefficient is easily obtained by dividing the drag force by the cross-sectional area and the dynamic air pressure $\frac{(\rho \times v^2)}{2}$, which equals q.

Drag coefficients of various shapes range from values as low as 0.05 for a pure airfoil to more than 1.0 for a flat plate or something designed to induce drag such as a parachute. The best ever car shape achieved to date was the wheel-driven world land speed record holder *Goldenrod*, with a recorded Cd of 0.1165, and the best production car to date is the 2-litre version of the Renault 25, with a Cd of 0.28. Formula 1 racing cars are designed to generate extremely high downforces and the induced drag and high turbulence from the exposed wheels give them drag coefficients in the 0.6 to 0.7 bracket. The current outright world land speed record holder *Thrust 2*, which generated 5000 lb of skin friction alone, has a Cd of around 0.4 (see Chapter 3 for more on record breakers).

Lift and downforce

The force acting vertically at right angles to the drag force is the aerodynamic lift force, and when a lateral component exists as well it is known as the side force. When the centre of aerodynamic pressure (the point through which the aerodynamic forces act) does not coincide with the centre of gravity, couples (or moments) are generated by the aerodynamic effects. Those about the X-axis are described as roll moments, those about the Y-axis as pitch moments and those about the Z-axis as yaw moments. In aerodynamic terms therefore a car body is subjected to six components of aerodynamic effect—three forces and three couples.

For simplified analysis, all mass inertia forces acting on a vehicle in motion are considered to be concentrated at the centre of gravity. In practice, they are more distributed and always divided in their ground reaction between the individual wheel contact patches. To determine the centre of pressure, aerodynamic moments are measured in a wind tunnel by the dynamic load changes in the balance readings, from which a virtual centre can be calculated. The lateral position should be very close to the centre line of car symmetry, while the vertical position is derived from the pitch moments and the longitudinal position from the yaw moments. These preliminary steps to determine the precise position of the centre of pressure are vital to all stability investigations.

At the centre of pressure there are, by definition, zero aerodynamic moments. But at any other point, moments exist which are derived from the distance and the force applied. In considering vehicle dynamics therefore, the aerodynamic moments about the centre of gravity are paramount and the relative positions of these two physical centres are very significant. In simplistic and general terms, a shape with the centre of pressure behind the centre of gravity (like a dart) is stable and a shape with the centre of pressure in front of the centre of gravity tends to be unstable. One of the aerodynamicist's most important tasks (see Chapter 5) is to develop dynamically stable vehicle characteristics from fine tuning the centre of pressure position.

Speed and scale effects: the 'Reynolds' Number'

It was Professor Osborne Reynolds of Manchester University who first formulated a way of comparing the conditions under which different fluids behaved in motion.

Cd of Simple Shapes

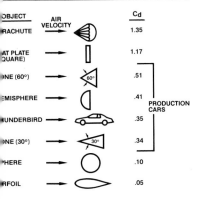

OBJECT	AIR VELOCITY	Cd
PARACHUTE		1.35
FLAT PLATE (SQUARE)		1.17
CONE (60°)		.51
HEMISPHERE		.41
THUNDERBIRD		.35
CONE (30°)		.34
SPHERE		.10
AIRFOIL		.05

PRODUCTION CARS

The drag coefficients of simple shapes range from 1.35 for a parachute to 0.05 for an optimized airfoil. US production cars span a bracket from just over 0.50 to about 0.32, while there are several European cars now below 0.30

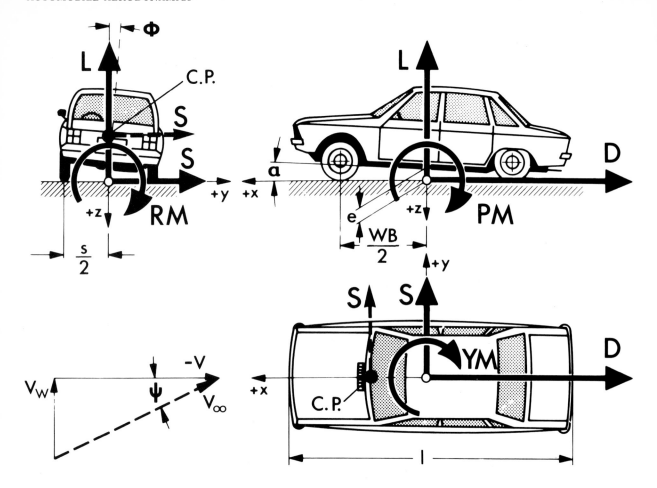

As well as the drag forces on a car, there are lift forces (L) and side forces (S) when there is a crosswind component (Vw) to the forward velocity (V). Due to the displacement of the centre of pressure (CP) from the centre of gravity, roll (RM), pitch (PM) and yaw moments (YM) are also generated

His paper to the Royal Society in 1883 set out a rule of fluid dynamic behaviour which is still very much used today, especially in the field of vehicle development, although at the time he was more concerned with the flow of liquids in pipes than the air flow over vehicle bodywork.

Reynolds' Number provides a useful way of compensating for scale and speed effects when making aerodynamic comparisons. It is a non-dimensional ratio obtained by multiplying the typical length of a body by its velocity and dividing by the kinematic coefficient of air viscosity.

Some body shapes display distinctly different flow patterns at different speeds. For this reason it is important to measure all aerodynamic characteristics over a wide range of air speeds. It does not always follow, for example, that a drag coefficient recorded at 60 mph will be maintained right through to the maximum speed of the vehicle, and lift or yaw effects sometimes increase suddenly and unexpectedly at a critical higher speed. These speed-related changes in the air flow pattern are frequently referred to as the 'Reynolds' effect'.

Side force and yaw effects

When the air stream is head on to a car, as when driving straight ahead in still air, the aerodynamic forces act only in a vertical plane as drag and lift. The resultant side forces are zero as the air flow splits symmetrically in the horizontal plane. In real life, however, conditions of perfectly still air are rare and because of tyre slip angles at high speed the car may not always be travelling precisely in the direction in which it is pointing.

The angle between the direction of motion and the direction of the air flow is known as the *yaw angle*. As soon as there is any degree of aerodynamic yaw angle on a car, the air flow becomes asymmetric and side effects are generated. For analysis these are resolved into three components of drag, lift and side forces acting through the aerodynamic centre of pressure.

Yaw angles and the resultant forces are most often caused by winds that are not exactly dead ahead or exactly dead astern. Any slight angle between the direction of motion and the direction of the wind forces generates side components and introduces yaw effects. In racing cars aerodynamic yaw effects are also generated by dynamic yaw effects like the drift angle during cornering, but in road cars such high speed driving conditions are extremely rare.

All crosswinds, therefore, whatever their component angle to the main air flow caused by the motion of the car, change the drag and lift forces and introduce side forces. A car travelling at 60 mph, for example, with a 90 degree cross wind of 10 mph is actually being subjected to an air flow with a yaw angle of about 9 degrees. And the same car moving at the same speed into a 45 degree diagonal wind of the same speed has an aerodynamic yaw angle of about 4 degrees. Increasing the wind speed to 30 mph in the same direction increases the yaw angle to about 12 degrees.

Reproducing crosswind conditions in a wind tunnel is a simple matter of turning the test model in relation to the air flow. Most tunnels are therefore built to include a turntable for the complete balance assembly and most wind tunnel tests are conducted throughout a range of different yaw angles. Obviously, an important part of car shape development is to minimize the effects of yaw angle changes on drag, lift and stability. Some designs, however, increase their drag coefficient by as much as 15 per cent at 10 degrees yaw angle in addition to the increase in frontal area caused by the exposure of side panels to the forward moving air stream. These changes are usually felt by the driver as a simple power reduction which restricts performance in windy conditions (the effects of transient side gusts will be dealt with separately in Chapter 5).

The amount of change introduced through yaw depends mostly on the drag coefficient of the car in profile. As a simple guide during early development a model can be tested completely at right angles to the air flow in a wind tunnel, and the shape refined to provide the optimum flow conditions. Although package constraints usually prevent much of the side area being reduced, conventional flow development can have a significant effect through small changes to bodywork details.

To indicate the orders of magnitude available to the aerodynamicist during development it is useful to know the results of wind tunnel comparisons of body surface features made by General Motors over 20 years ago. In relative tests on a simple 0.275 in. body gap between two panels, the surface drag at this point was more than halved by angling the forward edge downwards at 10 degrees and the rear edge upwards at 5 degrees. Dome-headed screws in place of hexagonal bolt heads cut the local surface drag by 60 per cent, while more shallow oval heads reduced it by 97 per cent on the hex-bolt starting level. A square-edged moulding at right angles to the air flow recorded twice the drag of a simple half-round section with the same 1:1 height/width ratio, while reducing the ratio to 0.5 reduced the local drag to under 1 per cent of the original value.

3 Speed record breakers through the years

Strange as it may seem at first glance, one of the earliest vehicles to hold the world land speed record in 1899 probably had a better drag coefficient than the fastest vehicle on wheels today, the *Project Thrust 2* jet-powered car. The reasons for this apparent lack of technological progress are as complex as they are fundamental to the whole essence of aerodynamics as a science.

To start at the beginning, even before the turn of the last century designers really knew pretty well that bluff bodies create more drag, that projected frontal area strongly influences wind resistance and that big spoked wheels were a major source of turbulence at high speed. As already explained, many pioneers took steps to reduce the source of all these forces in the general search for more speed and to raise the official land speed record in particular.

Electric power

In 1899 two men battled long and hard for the ultimate land speed honours, using every trick they knew to gain more speed and beat the best efforts of the other. One was a French nobleman, Le Comte Gaston de Chasseloup-Laubat, who in December 1898 was timed over a measured kilometre at St Germain, north of Paris, at 62.233 km/h (39.24 mph) in a large electric carriage built by Paris taxicab makers C. Jeantaud et Cie.

There followed a series of land speed record attempts, dominated by electric power which was more reliable and better developed than the internal combustion engine at this stage. Belgian racing driver Camille Jenatzy challenged Chasseloup-Laubat with a similar electric carriage built by the Compagnie Internationale des Transports Automobiles Electriques, and beat him. So the noble Comte returned to the fray with a new 'streamlined' body based on a slim shell mounted between the wheels, with a vertical knife-edge nose, tapered tail and smooth undertray. It was slab sided and perfectly flat on top, where the driver sat with only his feet inside the bodywork.

These changes from the more square-fronted earlier design allowed the same 36 hp electric motor to drive the machine up from its previous top speed of nearly 44 mph to 57.6 mph. It was a victory for aerodynamics, no matter how crudely executed, as much as for Chasseloup-Laubat and the Jeantaud taxi company.

Further inspired by the airships and marine torpedos of the 1890s, Camille Jenatzy then commissioned Carrosserie Rothschild of Paris to build him a more fully 'streamlined' body in aluminium alloy, to outdo his dreaded rival and hopefully push the record (now officially scrutinized by the Automobile Club of

France) beyond the magic metric 'ton' of 100 km/h. Aptly named *La Jamais Contente* (Never Satisfied), this torpedo-shaped machine took the record to 105.9 km/h (65.76 mph) and started a whole new styling trend.

Steam and petrol power

While electric power proved very attractive for urban based vehicles, the great horsepower race of the twentieth century started with steam and quickly moved into petrol as the main source of prime mover energy. When Leon Serpollet's steamer raised the world land speed record to over 75 mph on the Promenade des Anglais at Nice in 1902, it did so with a boat-like hull, pointed at both ends, and disc-covered wheels. And a month later Walter C. Baker took his enclosed Electric Torpedo to an unofficial 78 mph, followed by 104 mph in 1903 (see Chapter 1).

From this point on the petrol engine reigned almost supreme as larger and larger engines demanded larger and larger monsters to house them. There was little thought of streamlining as the official record climbed to over 100 mph in only two years. This was the era of road racing, with engines as large as 22.5 litres in the 1905 record-holding Darracq, where sheer engine power mattered more than road holding or aerodynamic drag.

But in 1905 the Stanley twins of Newton, Massachussets, started work on a record breaking special that was decades ahead of its time in aerodynamic concept. Like all Stanleys it was a steamer, with conventional boiler and double-acting twin-cylinder engine. But in mechanical layout it came close to a modern Grand Prix car, with the engine in the rear and the driver ahead of it.

Significantly, the driver sat on the floor of a body made from thin cedar strips covered with canvas and closely resembling an upturned canoe in appearance, with

The first land speed record holder in the world was Le Comte Gaston de Chasseloup-Laubat in this Jeantaud electric carriage. In 1898 he was timed at 62.233 km/h (39.24 mph)

39

*Leon Serpollet demonstrated
the superior performance of
steam as well as aero-
dynamics in 1902 when he
took the record to over 75 mph
on the Promenade at Nice
in this high, smooth-fronted
spring special*

little more than his head protruding. The underneath was completely filled in with a flat full-length underpan, while the semi-elliptic front and rear suspensions were also enclosed, together with the inboard rear-only brakes.

This car, known as the *Rocket* and driven by Fred Marriott, reached a top speed of 121.57 mph from an estimated 120 bhp in January 1906. The following year (with power boosted to about 156 bhp), when running at an estimated 132 mph on a further record attempt, it became airborne after hitting a gulley, flew briefly for 100 ft or so at a height of about 15 ft before crashing and being smashed to pieces. The intrepid driver escaped with surprisingly few injuries, but a primary aerodynamic principle had been clearly demonstrated.

The record-breaking monsters

More typical of the attention aerodynamics received during this period was the famous Benz *Blitzen*, a machine that was evolved in several stages eventually to reach an amazing 141.37 mph in one direction only on Daytona Beach, Florida, in 1911. This car was developed from the 1908 bluff-fronted Benz Grand Prix car, and followed similar lines in its original form.

In 1909 it broke through the 200 km/h barrier (124 mph) at Brooklands before being shipped back to the factory for a new more streamlined body. With a slimmed-down bonnet fitting so close to the 21.5-litre engine that the exhaust pipes were exposed on the left-hand side, and the gearlever and handbrake mounted outside the narrow cockpit, it went to Daytona Beach where it took the record (unofficially, as in one direction only) first to 131 mph in 1910 and then in 1911 to over 141 mph.

With World War 1 came two most important benefits that were subsequently applied to record-breaking car design. One was the development of supremely powerful aero engines, like the Packard V12 (later developed into the 'Liberty'). The other was a greater knowledge of aeronautical principles through the intensive war efforts in aviation. In some designs the large engine philosophy went hand-in-hand with attempts to provide a reasonably low-drag body as far as it could be

ABOVE *The famous Stanley brothers were extremely innovative – and years ahead of their time – when they built this record breaker, called the* Rocket, *in 1905. It closely resembled an inverted boat hull with a fully enclosed underbelly and is estimated to have exceeded 130 mph*

RIGHT *In 1928 Frank Lockhart built the extra-ordinary* Black Hawk Stutz, *with a 3-litre V-16 racing engine cooled by an ice tank and very low drag bodywork. He crashed to his death at about 225 mph when a rear tyre burst*

arranged to shroud at least one, and sometimes two, extremely large engines. In others, like the incredible *Black Hawk* Stutz, low drag was used to achieve remarkably high speeds from much more modest engines.

During the 1920s the official record rose from the 124 mph achieved at Brooklands in 1914 to over 200 mph, mainly through the use of brute force and aerodynamic ignorance. René Thomas used a little-modified Grand Prix Delage in 1922 to take speeds over 140 mph for the first time before the great British drivers—Malcolm Campbell, Henry Segrave and Parry Thomas—used a succession of aero-engined monsters to reach over 206 mph in 1928. That was the year of the ill-fated *White Triplex Special*, with three 27-litre Liberty engines and 1400 bhp on tap, and the first time low drag became an intrinsic feature of record-breaking design.

The car that changed the direction of events was known as the *Black Hawk* Stutz and designed by a young Indianapolis driver called Frank Lockhart. It was based on the dominant Miller racing cars of the mid 1920s and used a 3-litre V16 engine built from two racing straight eights to develop 385 bhp at 7500 rpm. Its chassis and bodywork were dedicated to low drag for high speed, with inboard suspension, fully shrouded wheels housed in detached nacelle-shaped fairings and a sealed engine compartment using an ice tank for cooling. Even the exhaust stubs finished flush with the body surface.

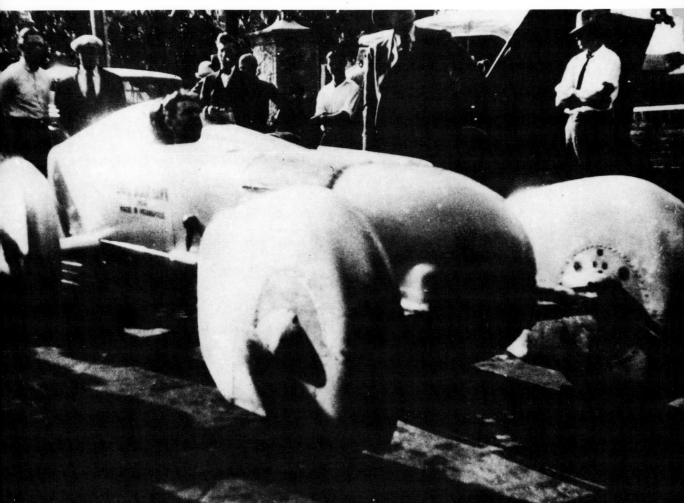

Malcolm Campbell and Bluebird were synonymous with record-breaking speeds for more than a decade as he took the record from 200 to over 300 mph. These three Bluebirds (left 1928, below left 1932, below 1935) show how the aerodynamics of the car developed from an open-wheeled monster into a more enclosed envelope

Such enterprise and 'clean' aerodynamic styling, which extended to a full belly underpan and a faired-in front axle, should have paid off handsomely for the pioneering Lockhart, but the deficiencies of using instinct rather than sound technical knowledge inevitably caused problems. First the engine was starved of air through the flush surface intakes and, finally, when entering the timing straight at about 225 mph a rear tyre burst. The car skidded and somersaulted before Lockhart was thrown out to his death.

Campbell's Bluebird

Also in 1928 came a major redesign of Malcolm Campbell's *Bluebird*, which was boosted to over 500 bhp and fitted with a more efficient body, using fairings to reduce tyre drag, surface radiators at the rear and a tail fin for the first time. It took the record to 206.956 mph and was quickly followed by Henry Segrave's 925 bhp Napier-engined *Golden Arrow*, which used a pencil-thin body with tailored sponsons between front and rear wheels and an even larger tail fin. In 1929 *Golden Arrow* achieved 231.446 mph.

In 1931 Campbell returned with another *Bluebird* redesign, using a 1450 bhp Napier Lion aero engine and a much more aerodynamic body nearly 30 ft in length with a fully ducted front radiator and a huge stabilizing tail fin. This car took the record to 246 mph before being fitted with a 2300 bhp Rolls-Royce V12 which in 1933 boosted it to an amazing 272.46 mph.

Bluebird's designer, Reid Railton, then took a totally fresh look at the most efficient shape envelope for a new record attempt in 1935. He chose a new full-width body, working on the theory that the reduced tyre drag would more than compensate for the increased frontal area. The radiator was fed through a wide, shallow nose duct, exhausting over the bonnet top well ahead of the engine, and fitted with a manually-operated blanking shutter to reduce drag during the 12 seconds it took to cover the measured mile. The car weighed 5 tons, including lead ballast at the rear to alleviate wheelspin on the beaches used for record-breaking runs. After setbacks at Daytona, Campbell moved to the Bonneville Salt Flats, where *Bluebird* eventually reached an average of 301.129 mph.

In automotive terms, *Bluebird* was probably the last of the great world land speed record cars. From that point in history on, not only the engines came from high-speed aircraft but much of the body features as well. Aerodynamic design turned to the fast advancing field of aviation for its inspiration, as first George Eyston and then John Cobb took the record up to nearly 400 mph in 1947 in a succession of machines that could in no way be related to road vehicles, or even provide spin-off technology of use to the motor industry.

Mercedes-Benz Type 80

In 1936, shortly after Malcolm Campbell had taken the world land speed record through the 300 mph barrier so convincingly on the Bonneville Salt Flats, a remarkable German project got under way to bring back the outright honours to the fatherland. It was to use one of the latest Daimler-Benz 1300 bhp aero engines being developed for Heinkel bombers. It was to be driven by its main instigator, racing driver Hans Stuck; it was to be designed by Ferdinand Porsche and built by the Mercedes-Benz Competition Department in Stuttgart.

The mechanical configuration followed Porsche's Auto Union Grand Prix

Henry Segrave's Golden Arrow *(below) and George Eyston's* Thunderbolt *(right) also took records in the late 1920s in competition with Campbell. It was the quest for higher speeds that led to these 1000 bhp monsters turning into what progressively resembled wingless aircraft*

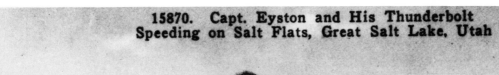

15870. Capt. Eyston and His Thunderbolt
Speeding on Salt Flats, Great Salt Lake, Utah

Built just before World War 2 as the ultimate low-drag record breaker, the Mercedes-Benz Type 80 never ran. It showed how drag coefficients on this type of car could be lowered to below 0.20, with a scale model actually recording 0.18, and was one of the first cars to use inverted airfoils to generate downforce

conception of an engine mounted behind the driver, ahead of the rear wheels, for the best traction and a low drag, easy penetration nose. To reduce tyre loadings at high speed and improve traction off the line, tandem rear axles were fitted with the wheels packaged against a vast clutch housing (track width was only 51 in.), to keep the body slim.

In aerodynamic terms the design, known as experimental Type 80, was highly innovative in many unusual ways. It used stub wings (about 30 in. long with a maximum chord width of close to 5 ft) each side of the body with inverted airfoil section and negative angle of attack, to generate downforce through the centre of gravity. During development a rear airfoil on struts with an adjustable angle of attack was also proposed, as was a pair of self-stabilizing fins on the front corners of the body, trimmed automatically by a central vane and links, operating like trim tabs on an aircraft's control surfaces.

Early tests showed that the Cd of a scale model, designed to hug the mechanical components and wheels as tightly as possible, was about 0.18 and that the frontal area was about 1.7 sq. m. The underside was fully enclosed with radiator and oil

cooling arranged through a wide duct under the nose which exhausted further back under the car.

By the time the Type 80 was ready to roll, war had broken out and its experimental 44.5-litre DB 603 aero engine was needed for other things. In its later stage of development, the Type 80 could certainly have taken the world speed record to at least 400 mph with a post-war 3000 bhp version of the engine fitted, but German industry by then was in ruins and could ill afford such diversions. The car today stands almost unnoticed in the Mercedes Stuttgart Museum.

And there the record-breaking story might have stopped, had not a band of American drivers started the race all over again in the early 1960s with jet engines and rocket motors running in little less than cropped-wing aircraft fuselages. Eventually Gary Gabelich, using 58,000 lb of thrust in his 38 ft long rocket-powered *Blue Flame*, broke 630 mph in 1970 before the sponsors lost interest and the money for record breaking ran out.

Class records: science takes priority

As long as there were no specific design restrictions on the absolute land speed record, it was always easier to gain speed by sheer brute force. And with aviation power units reaching higher and higher bounds to the point where even space rocket motors might become available, the land speed record enthusiasts did not need to consider low drag a priority.

It was further down the scale, where engine size at least provided a serious constraint, that far more scientific effort was applied to record breaking and where the role of aerodynamics became the main priority for success. As mentioned in Chapter 1, there was considerable activity in the field of record attempts in Nazi Germany shortly before World War 2. The duel for honours between the two national sporting marques—Mercedes and Auto Union—led to rapid advances and some outstanding achievements.

Provided some kind of record could be claimed expense and effort were not spared to demonstrate the supremacy of German technology, which in this field at least proved to be more developed an in any other part of the world. While Campbell's *Bluebird* and Eyston's *Thunderbolt* were striving to break 350 mph with thousands of aero horsepower on the Florida beaches, the Germans applied the very best in aerodynamics to their modified Grand Prix cars to reach 250 mph from only 600 bhp on closed sections of public road.

Such is the nature of laminar air flow that the car Mercedes developed in 1939 by fitting an all enveloping body to their W154 Grand Prix machine had many features similar to the ill-fated *Black Hawk* Stutz that had killed Frank Lockhart on Daytona Beach in 1928. Both cars were front-engined and cooled by ice tanks to eliminate the drag-inducing need for a front radiator opening. Both cars used fully enclosed wheel fairings, outrigged from a slim central fuselage body with enclosed suspension and a full-length smooth underpan. But the Stutz had been an instinctive design, highly innovative for its day and a clever application of aircraft concepts, while the Mercedes was meticulously developed empirically in a wind tunnel.

From the start of their record-breaking efforts the Mercedes motor sport engineers had been devising ways to reduce drag, not just on the record breakers but also on the Grand Prix cars and even production vehicles. Typical bluff-fronted competition cars at that time had Cd values in the 0.6–0.8 bracket*, so there was

*These Cd values were proved as recently as 1982 when *Autocar* magazine put a 1933 Bugatti Type 51 in the MIRA wind tunnel for drag and lift tests. It recorded a Cd of 0.74 with a frontal area of only 14 sq. ft and a negative rear lift coefficient, probably caused by the leverage effect of its brick-shaped front and teardrop tail.

49

plenty of room for improvement. Tests undertaken in 1937 on a one-fifth scale model showed that full wheel covers could cut the Cd of the W125 Grand Prix car from 0.599 to only 0.293.

Later the same year some further models, to a slightly larger one-quarter scale, were also tunnel tested and developed to reduce the drag coefficient even further to a value of only 0.184. When combined with the extremely small frontal area of 14 sq. ft, this gave a CdA value of only 0.246 which is less than half that of the most aerodynamically advanced production car today.

Even further down the size scale there were some quite remarkable British achievements made by MG record breakers in the 1930s as well. Major 'Goldie' Gardner, using a streamlined body designed by Reid Railton and a supercharged 1-litre 6-cylinder engine, managed over 200 mph in 1939 in the MG EX135. The same car was later developed into the EX179 with a Cd value around 0.20 and fitted with various engines to take many other records in several under 2-litre classes.

Transonic jet power

With ten successful American world speed record attempts completed between 1964 and 1970 taking speeds well into the transonic range at 630.388 mph, it was a bold British dream of one Richard Noble to bring the record back to the UK. But he set about establishing a decidedly shoestring operation in a very professional way towards the end of 1977 and, despite all manner of setbacks, achieved the 'impossible' in 1983 when *Project Thrust 2* set a new world record of 633.468 mph.

The attempt started on the drawing board with a full appreciation of the aerodynamics involved. At the hottest time of day in Bonneville, with an ambient temperature of 24 degrees Celsius, the peak speed reached during the 6-mile run-in of 650 mph represents a Mach Number of 0.84, well inside the transonic range where surface drag rises dramatically—in this case to more than 40 per cent of the

BELOW *By 1939 record breaking had become well established in all kinds of different categories. For Major 'Goldie' Gardner a series of MG specials like this EX135 advanced the state of the aerodynamic art in a series of leaps and bounds. Its low frontal area and smooth skin allowed it to reach more than 200 mph*

RIGHT *After World War 2, in 1957, the same basic car (see above), updated with an even lower drag body envelope to become the EX179, returned to the Salt Flats to take more class records*

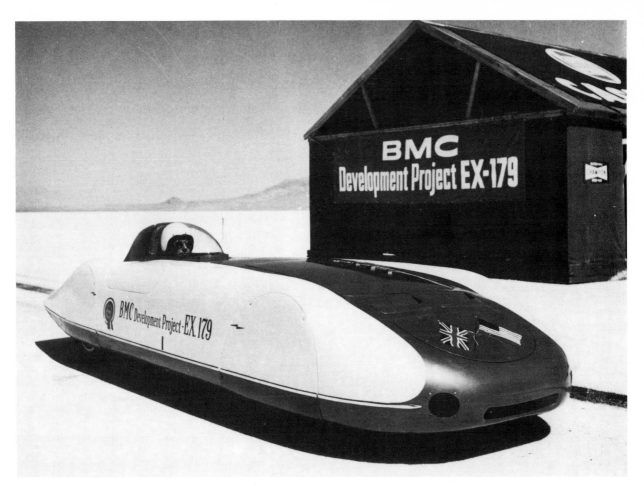

total. So after a rolling chassis was constructed to house the 30,000 bhp reheated Rolls-Royce Avon gas turbine, it was clothed in a smooth aerodynamic body that was first tested as a one tenth scale model in the British Aerospace low speed wind tunnel at Bristol.

To investigate the significance of ground effects likely to be caused by the boundary layer between the smooth underpan and the dried mud surface, further tests were then conducted in the moving floor tunnel at Southampton University before a one-thirtieth scale model machined from solid aluminium was built for testing in the British Aerospace transonic tunnel at Weybridge. Apart from confirmation that the drag was sufficiently low to allow the 16,800 lb of engine thrust to drive the car to its design speed, the aerodynamic objectives were to confirm lift coefficients and stability characteristics as acceptable.

Contrary to what might be expected, *Thrust 2* was designed for zero lift and zero downforce. Too much lift would obviously cause steering problems and a risk of the car taking off at speed. Too much downforce would cause the solid tyres to dig into the lake bed. During test runs the downforces were monitored through linear transducers measuring front suspension displacement and the car trimmed by changing the angle of incidence.

What happens to a car in these exceedingly high speed brackets bears no relationship to anything likely to be encountered at road speeds, but the science involved is nevertheless an interesting part of the aerodynamics story. Forces

created by the air flow around the body and by the wheels especially cause peculiar effects which were well predicted by the engineers responsible for the *Thrust 2* design.

The solid aluminium alloy rear tyres used for the record runs were specially machined with a shallow vee section designed to act like a power boat hull and lift up on to the 'plane' above 240 mph. This was intended to reduce rolling drag on the relatively soft surface and also allow sideways skidding should control be lost without the tyres digging in and flipping the car over. Their covers had to withstand sonic shocks on their outer surface and a ballooning typhoon inside the wheelhouse. Sonic shock waves off the front wheels were found to dam the underbody air flow, sharply reducing the venturi effect and hence the downforce above 550 mph. This phenomenon was used to advantage by increasing the angle of incidence of the car from zero to a nose up inclination of 10 minutes, so that wheel drag was reduced and more speed achieved.

According to the traces recorded on the actual record runs, the maximum downforce of 1200 lb at 450 mph reduced to zero at 600 mph and turned to 2040 lb of lift at 650 mph. This cut the load on the front wheels from 6360 to 3680 lb, with a proportional reduction in rolling drag.

The other unusual effect of *Thrust 2* aerodynamics related to stability and the way this was controlled. Although rudder-assisted steering was considered, vertical control surfaces were confined to a pair of tail fins, swept back and tapered. Twin fins were chosen to reduce the height of the roll moment induced by their area. Dynamic stability was provided by 6 degrees front castor angle and differential 'tread' patterns for front and rear wheels.

ABOVE *Between 1964 and 1970 there were ten successful world speed record attempts in the USA, culminating in Gary Gabelich's rocket-powered* Blue Flame *tricycle which achieved just over 630 mph in 1970*

Thrust's outer skin was fabricated in alloy and aerospace reinforced plastic, flush-riveted and bonded to a square-tube frame built up on a massive skeleton structure reinforced with webs and bulkheads. Including the 'single spool' gas turbine which developed 16,800 lb of thrust at sea level, the total car weighed just under 9000 lb with 64 per cent over the front wheels. To help relieve the enormous heat developed in the reheat pipe, a ventilation system was developed using the natural upper surface shape to generate intakes feeding a cooling flow around the tailpipe.

On 4 October 1983 Richard Noble ran *Thrust* 2 just 0.88 mph over its design speed and during all his record attempts exceeded 600 mph eleven times, which is more than any land speed record car has ever done before. He set six official new speed records with a car that achieved everything its designer, aerospace engineer John Ackroyd, expected of it in every mechanical and aerodynamic detail in a ground speed regime where very few men had previously travelled.

To complete the fastest land vehicle story it must be recorded that the fastest man on wheels is not Richard Noble. American stunt driver Stan Barrett has held this honour since 1979 after running briefly above Mach 1 at 739. 66 mph in a machine called the *Budweiser Special*, powered by rocket and a Sidewinder missile power pack.

BELOW *The American efforts inspired Richard Noble to bring the record back to Britain with his* Project Thrust 2, *a highly-developed aerodynamic four-wheeled jet car that eventually reached over 633 mph in 1983*

Mercedes-Benz came back in 1979 with this unusual development of their C111 experimental coupé. It ran first with a 5-cylinder turbo diesel engine developing 230 bhp, then with a twin-turbo petrol V8 producing 500 bhp. The running drag coefficient was 0.195 and the top speed around 250 mph. Note the asymmetric rear wings to counter the centrifugal air spillage on the banked clockwise track

Another kind of land speed record

In terms of ultimate achievement, these outright accomplishments in the USA completely overshadowed another just as worthy land speed record taken at the Nardo proving ground in southern Italy, by a very special Volkswagen diesel car. Designed as an aerodynamic research vehicle to investigate the problems of lift and stability at very low drag coefficients, the ARVW (Aerodynamic Research Volkswagen) sustained 214.26 mph over 500 km from a standing start, with a fastest lap at 224.98 mph. It was powered by a turbocharged 6-cylinder diesel (with charge-air cooling), developing 175 bhp in a sleek fully-enclosed body with a Cd of only 0.15. It became the fastest diesel car in the world, an honour previously held by a specially cut-down 1972 Opel GT.

Records of a completely different type were taken by this Volkswagen diesel-powered research vehicle which not only reached over 224 mph but achieved a drag coefficient of only 0.15

4 Wind tunnels and how they work

By definition, a wind tunnel is a controlled test environment where aerodynamic effects can be studied using an artificial air flow. Within this context, probably the first example of this particular science dates from Benjamin Robins' advanced ballistics experiments as early as 1746. His technique was to fire a variety of different shaped bullets and musket balls at a heavy wooden pendulum and compare the efficiency of their aerodynamics in flight by the distance it moved. Robins was a mathematician, well able to calculate velocity from energy and mass.

At that time, of course, there was no convenient source of power to drive test equipment. The steam engine had not yet been developed. So, to advance his technique, Robins devised a piece of apparatus that was to prove very significant in later years—the whirling arm. Through the latter half of the eighteenth century, scientists like Richard Edgeworth and John Smeaton developed more advanced versions of the same idea, designed to measure the resistance of bodies through the air by whirling them round on a rotating arm.

Sir George Cayley brought the whirling arm to its peak in 1804, with a version clearly sketched in his experimental notes and fully described in his famous and pioneering 1809 essay on 'aerial navigation'. It comprised a tripod stand supporting a vertical axle on which was mounted the horizontal arm. It was driven by a cord wound round the lower end of the axle, passed over a pulley and attached to a 1 lb weight. At one end of the arm, which measured about five feet in length and was constructed as a light framework with minimum air resistance, a rectangular plate exactly 12 in. square was mounted. At the other it was counterbalanced by a small lead weight.

His experiment was to time the rotation of the arm over 20 revolutions, equivalent to about 600 feet of linear movement of the plate, and calculate the speed generated from the known input of 1 lb force. He was looking for a relationship between air resistance and speed and concluded that for a pressure of 1 lb/sq. in. on a flat plate at right angles to the air flow, the median speed was 23.6 ft/sec. Cayley also calculated the speed generated at different angles of incidence and he even noted that the air density could affect the accuracy of his results.

The step from whirling arms to proper wind tunnels took another 60 years to make, when a group of keen aeronautically inclined engineers founded the Aeronautical Society (later the Royal Aeronautical Society) in London in 1866. Francis Wenham, a marine engineer, together with John Browning built the first wind tunnel there in 1870 'to obtain data on which a true science of aeronautics can be founded'. It was made of wood and measured about 10 ft long by 18 in. square.

Two years later, a Frenchman called E.J. Marey developed rapid-sequence

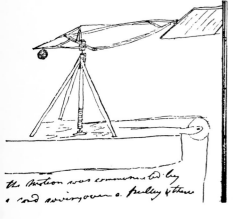

This sketch taken from Sir George Cayley's actual notes shows the primitive whirling arm he used in 1804 to measure drag forces on a variety of wing shapes

The first known aerodynamic test equipment was this swinging pendulum built by Benjamin Robins in 1746 to measure the ballistics of musket balls, fired into its wooden block

photography to capture the wing activities of birds in flight. Marey went on to devise a technique for photographing air flow patterns in wind tunnels using smoke trails, a visualization process still used today.

By the turn of the century the race was on all round the world to achieve sustained and controlled winged flight. There were gliders making short straight-line hops, there were free-flight balloons and powered airships taking some remarkable endurance records, but a true understanding of lift forces on wings and the science of control surfaces had not yet been reached.

In Dayton, Ohio, two young men, who had failed to make a viable success of a small-town local newspaper, turned to the booming bicycle business for a livelihood. In 1892, Wilbur and Orville Wright opened a small shop, hiring and repairing the new-fangled pedal-driven machines that were bringing individual low-cost transportation on an unprecedented scale. The engineering skills this business brought were to prove invaluable in future years.

Wilbur Wright became obsessed with not just a desire to fly, but a desire to fly in a machine that could be controlled properly by the pilot. He deduced very early in his first gliding experiments that balance and control of aerodynamic surfaces were essential to the success of any flying machine. And he was a stickler for the systematic approach.

In 1901 Wilbur Wright conducted his first controlled aerodynamic tests on a wing section, mounted conveniently on an old bicycle wheel running horizontally in an open field on a windy day. There were too many variations in wind speed and too many gusts for any sensible results, so he mounted the same apparatus on a framework above the front wheel of a bicycle and pedalled it steadily through still air at a constant speed.

The results were significant enough for him to know that the only hope of building an effective flying machine lay in further and meticulously controlled tests. So he converted an old starch box about 18 in. long into an open trough and blew air through from one end to the other. Inside he set up a piece of equipment that was to become a vital tool in his researches—a modified weather vane.

From his bicycle wheel tests, Wilbur Wright knew that the lift forces on a flat plate changed with its angle of incidence to the air flow. What he needed to develop was a relationship between lift and the plate's proportions (the aspect ratio, or length/chord dimensions) and what he needed to investigate was the effect of curvature and plate profile (the section shape) on lift efficiency. His primitive aerodynamic balance used a flat plate at one end of a freely pivoting arm and an adjustable and replaceable test section at the other. The angle this arm adopted in his 'tunnel' therefore measured the lift generated by the section.

In the chronology of wind tunnel history, it should also be recorded that independently at the same time Dr A.F. Zahm built one of the first full-sized tunnels in Washington, DC. It had a test section 16 ft square and measured about 40 ft in length with a 5 ft diameter suction fan drawing air through at speeds up to 27 mph. But Zahm's tunnel was insignificant compared to what was achieved by the Wright brothers' efforts when they constructed their second tunnel in their bicycle workshop later the same year.

The second Wright wind tunnel was a much more ambitious affair, based on the experience of other early aerodynamicists. It was slightly smaller than that built over 30 years previously by Francis Wenham, but similar. The test section was 16 in. square and the overall length about 6 ft. It was made of wood as a free-standing structure and particularly significant for two special reasons: it used a funnel-shaped diffuser to concentrate and accelerate the air flow across the test section and it used a series of grids and mesh screens to straighten and balance the air flow so that it was as uniform as possible. Both these features are critical to the proper functioning of all modern wind tunnels.

As there was no electricity in the bicycle workshop, a small gas engine was used to drive a two-bladed fan. And to maintain steady-state conditions as accurately as possible, nothing in the workshop was allowed to be moved once tests had started. During the testing, Wilbur always adopted the same position, observing readings through a glass inspection window on a dial pointer at the bottom of the balance pivot. Using a simple vane with the test wing removed, the Wrights spent nearly a month stabilizing the air flow through the test section until, in their own words 'it did not vary by more than one-eighth of a degree'.

Once set up, the equipment was used to test some 150 to 200 model wings according to a schedule that involved two distinct stages. Over five laborious weeks all kinds of wings were cut by hand from $\frac{1}{32}$ in. steel sheet with shears and carefully shaped to different profiles. From these initial results a second test programme was developed to find the optimum airfoil shape, during which some fundamental effects of incidence angle and chord curvature were discovered for the first time.

The tables of values which resulted, containing several thousand empirical measurements of wing performance, were kept a closely guarded secret for many years. They were fundamental to the Wrights' first successful powered flights, and were far in advance of any contemporary research work. As late as 1939, well after the era of regular commercial airliner travel had already dawned, the first qualified aeronautical engineer was allowed detailed access to the Wrights' results. He declared these to be amazingly accurate and incredibly comprehensive in their grasp of fundamental aerodynamic principles.

The application of wind tunnels to automotive design work came not long after the Wright brothers' pioneering efforts in their second wind tunnel, faithfully reconstructed in the late 1930s under the direction of Orville Wright and presently to be seen in the Henry Ford Museum, Dearborn, Michigan. But the connection with aviation resulted more from airships than winged aircraft, mainly through the work of Count Zeppelin, who successfully pioneered air travel in a form that remained viable until well into the thirties.

In his early researches into the optimum profile and aspect ratio for airships, Count Zeppelin employed a young engineer called Paul Jaray, who studied aerodynamics at the Technical College of Prague from 1907 to 1910. Jaray was instrumental in the design of Zeppelin airships, which he transformed from their original long, thin profile to a blunter shape about five times as long as it was fat at its maximum section.

In 1916, Jaray persuaded Zeppelin to build a wind tunnel. It was 3 ft in diameter with a 218 bhp engine driving a four-blade propeller generating speeds up to 124 mph. The following year, he built a bigger and better tunnel, the largest at that time in Germany, with a 10 ft test section diameter and a split return. It was this tunnel that he later used for his pioneering experiments on low-drag automotive shapes.

At the end of World War 1, when German aircraft firms were prevented from further development in the aviation field, Jaray turned to car design, using the Zeppelin tunnel to test out his advanced aerodynamic theories. The size of the tunnel was still too small for full scale models to be used, so Jaray used one-tenth scale wooden mock-ups suspended from wires. He set out to prove that the basic

The Wright brothers' early wind tunnel was reconstructed under Orville's supervision in the 1930s, using an electric fan to blow air through a rectangular box in which he originally tested hundreds of different wing sections (from the collections of Greenfield Village and the Henry Ford Museum, Dearborn, Michigan)

shape of a car has much more influence on its total drag than any amount of detail streamlining, and he proved it by his remarkable achievement of only 0.28 drag coefficient (his figure which later proved to be an even lower 0.245) on a fully detailed but enclosed-bottom saloon.

In France, Alexandre Gustav Eiffel, after he had built his famous tower in 1899 (and had used it incidentally for early aerodynamic experiments in the open environment to be found almost 1000 ft above the Paris streets), constructed a wind tunnel. Like its predecessors, it was of the open circuit straight-flow type, drawing air in one end and exhausting it the other. Facilities of this type, which are still in common use, are known as Eiffel-type tunnels.

Germany remained at the forefront of wind tunnel development and in the design of aerodynamic shapes right through the thirties. The University of Göttingen built a new kind of tunnel with a closed circuit for the air flow, which recirculated through the system. Tunnels of this type recover some of the fan energy, saving power, reducing noise and allowing the air temperature and humidity to be maintained at constant levels. They take up more space, however, and cost more to build. They are known as the Göttingen type and are now widely used in automotive development today.

The most advanced aerodynamic development on car shapes was undertaken in 1930 by an organization affiliated to the Stuttgart Technical High School and known as the Motor Vehicle Research Institute. Some 300 staff were employed by the MVRI using two tunnels, both designed specifically for automotive work. Scale model testing was carried out in a small round-section tunnel with a moving floor, while full-size models were investigated in a much larger D-section tunnel. Its throat measured 17 ft by 24 ft and a 5500 bhp fan provided air speeds up to 180 mph.

Both the Stuttgart and Göttingen tunnels were significantly instrumental in the development of Mercedes and BMW sports and racing cars during the 1930s and played a key role in the resurgence of the German car industry after World War 2. It was only in 1974 that Mercedes-Benz completed its own exclusive wind tunnel at Sindelfingen, eight years after Volkswagen's tunnel was constructed in Wolfsburg.

Altogether a total of 12 full-scale automotive wind tunnels has been built over the past 25 years in Europe, with three more in North America and four in Japan. Fifteen are owned by car manufacturers and operated by their development departments as a valuable in-house facility. One is owned by an aircraft company, the remainder by research institutes. Each is fully utilized during the working day, some around the clock.

Prior to 1960 there were very few full-size tunnels. One existed at the Aerotechnical Institute of St Cyr near Paris, others at the Turin Polytechnic University, the National Physical Laboratory in England, the Stockholm Technical University, Sweden (where Saab developed their aerodynamic 1947 Model 92) and at the Dutch National Aeronautical Laboratory, Amsterdam, Netherlands.

In the USA a whole series of small-scale wind tunnels was built in 1926 after a $2.5 million fund was set up by one Daniel Guggenheim, for the promotion of aeronautics. One of the most significant in automotive terms, naturally enough, was constructed by the University of Detroit to investigate quarter scale model behaviour with both fixed and moving floor planes. Close by in Ann Arbor, the University of Michigan built a tunnel for original work on fundamental car shapes.

In 1934, at the Guggenheim Aeronautical Laboratory of Stanford University, Elliot G. Reid tried to develop an 'ideal' car shape using one-fifth scale models in the newly-constructed wind tunnel. Within the package constraints of a typical 1933 five-passenger saloon (with a 127 in. wheelbase), two of his graduate students—D.B. Bates and E.F. Stoner—developed four aerodynamic models which they proved could save between 19 and 55 per cent of the power required to drive them at speeds between 20 and 60 mph.

Optimistically, as it turned out, Reid predicted in a paper presented to the Society of Automotive Engineers in January 1935 that 'rapid obsolescence of the present or "horseless carriage" type would follow the appearance of streamlined, rear-engine motor cars'. At Ohio State University a series of tests were also carried out in a 3 ft diameter tunnel to investigate drag influences between 35 and 55 mph. And in 1937 actual tests were made to determine the effects of tail fins on side wind stability at the National Bureau of Standards.

After World War 2 a new tunnel was built at the University of Wichita, Kansas, with a test section measuring 7 ft by 10 ft in which some spurious measurements were made on full-size cars. But the real importance of aerodynamics to the US car industry never came until the 1970s, when there was intense government pressure to meet legislated fuel targets (see Chapter 8). Amazingly to the European eye, the world's largest car producers—General Motors—built their first dedicated automotive wind tunnel as late as 1980, while Ford US axed their plans for an automotive tunnel before the foundations had been completed.

Yet there was a keen interest in the effects of aerodynamics much earlier in the history of the American automotive industry. In 1932 it suddenly became fashionable to promote new models through aerodynamics, although little was really known about the science at that time. The objective was to make last year's cars obsolete and generate a larger replacement market at a time when sales had crashed by over 75 per cent in only three years.

An American auto industry newsletter dated May/June 1932 identified a new theme: 'The resistance of automobile bodies at high speed and its effect on car performance and economy is a subject much discussed at present. Higher average driving speeds made possible by improved roads and better engines make the problem of overcoming air resistance of great importance.'

In response, Chrysler began testing car shapes in a wind tunnel of their own, developing the most advanced yet commercially unsaleable 8-cylinder Airflow in 1934. Its smooth front and shrouded rear wheels were the direct product of wind tunnel work, but failed to bring any perceived customer benefits, so in 1937 it was phased out.

Concern at Ford over what might be presented in the market against their 1933 Lincoln V8 resulted in some original air flow visualization using quarter scale models in 'one of the leading University wind tunnels'. In addition to smoke tests

1934 CHRYSLER AIRFLOW

Aerodynamics became a powerful marketing tool as early as 1932 in the USA, with a succession of supposedly low drag bodystyles, like this 1934 Chrysler Airflow, from all the big producers

Half models of a 1933 Ford Lincoln were mounted on a flat white lacquered plate, covered in a coating of lamp black and kerosene. The air flow then caused the kerosene to cut through the soot, revealing the stream-lines. Note the effects of the sunvisor and vertical screen angle (below)

using a small moveable nozzle and a motion picture camera, a coating of lamp black (soot) and kerosene was applied to a white lacquered plate on which was mounted a half-model of the car. With the plate and model horizontal (to eliminate any gravity effects in the fluid), the air flow then caused the kerosene to score through the soot along the streamlines and evaporate, revealing the white surface beneath and creating a permanent record of the flow pattern.

Tests were carried out at speeds from 50 to 90 mph and the claim was made that the Lincoln was an efficient 'Air Flow' design that could eliminate wind resistance and provide the following advantages:

1 Less horsepower required for a given speed.
2 Less fuel consumption.
3 Reduction of air noise due to the smooth flow over and around the body.
4 Reduction of air turbulence and, therefore, improved stability at high speeds.'

In the light of the bluff front and flat vertical windscreen, these tests can only appear now to have been a desperate, but in the event effective, anti-propaganda measure designed to spike the Chrysler guns before the Airflow hit the streets.

61

Wind tunnels in use today

Automotive wind tunnels can be subdivided in several ways. There are scale-model wind tunnels in which early development of shape and detail for new models takes place as a valuable stage in arriving at an optimum and efficient design. There are also a few non-aerodynamic full-size wind tunnels, where cooling systems, heaters, wiper performance and other vehicle functions are developed in a simulated air flow on a rolling road or chassis dynamometer under engine load. These climatic or environmental tunnels are discussed later (see Chapter 6).

Fully aerodynamic wind tunnels are fitted with accurate measuring devices for determining all the forces generated on a vehicle by the air stream. They provide stable linear flow through the test chamber and often include a means of rotating the model in the horizontal plane to simulate yaw conditions like those derived from driving on a motorway in a cross wind.

The Volkswagen wind tunnel at Wolfsburg is unique in having a movable test section cover for converting it into an environmental chamber where vehicle systems can be developed under controlled ambient conditions

Before the two successive energy crises of the 1970s, vehicle aerodynamics was not a major consideration in the development of the passenger car. There was therefore only a very limited number of automotive wind tunnels available for full scale testing and the results obtained during the development of a new model were not of general public interest. Each company therefore had its own wind tunnel data base by which improvements and aerodynamic performance were measured. There was then no real reason for correlation with other data bases.

But the increased importance of fuel efficiency changed all that. Suddenly it

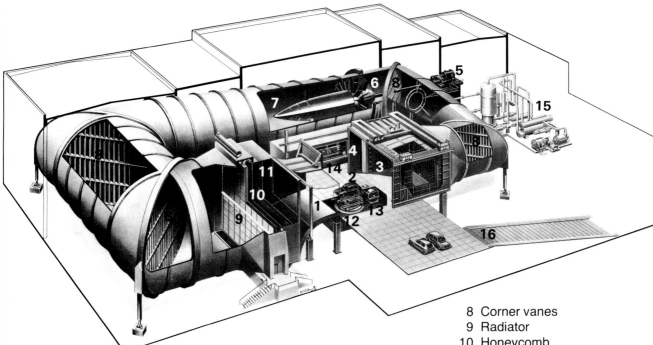

1 Nozzle
2 Test section
3 Collector
4 Movable test section cover
5 Electrical drive with transmission
6 Fan
7 Diffuser

8 Corner vanes
9 Radiator
10 Honeycomb
11 Turbulence screens
12 Balance
13 Roller dynamometer
14 Control room, process control computer
15 Refrigeration plant
16 Access to test section

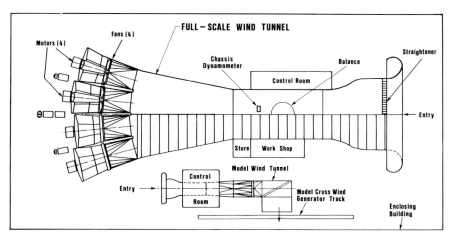

Britain's Motor Industry Research Association tunnel at Nuneaton is an open-circuit Eiffel design, with a closed test section. It is one of the very few full-scale automotive facilities in the UK and in almost constant use

seemed that absolute drag coefficients would make worthwhile marketing platforms for advanced new models and, for any sort of valid comparison to be made, correction factors between tunnels became of paramount importance. The construction rate of new tunnels worldwide therefore went up. In the 30 years between 1944 and 1974, nine new automotive tunnels were built and commissioned. Between 1975 and 1985, ten more have been completed.

In size the full-scale tunnels in use today for car development range from the vast aircraft installation belonging to the National Research Council of Canada in Ottawa, with a nozzle area of more than 893 sq. ft to the tiny Volvo tunnel in Gothenburg, with only 42 sq. ft. There are open-circuit Eiffel types (used by the Japanese and by the Motor Industry Research Association in England) and closed-circuit Göttingen types (used by most European car makers who need the environmental control for vehicle system development as well as aerodynamic investigation).

As well as different air flow circuits, tunnels are categorized by another key distinction in the design of the actual test area. Those where this part of the installation is enclosed by walls which come in contact with the air flow are known as closed-section tunnels. Those where there is no wall within reach of the air flow in the proximity of the test model are known as open-section tunnels. Intermediate designs using slotted walls which prevent some boundary layer effects are known as semi-open tunnels.

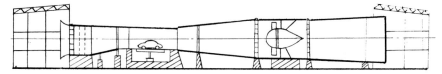

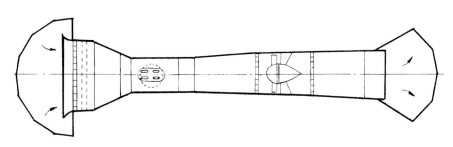

RIGHT Nissan also use an open-circuit Eiffel-type tunnel in Japan, with atmospheric air drawn over the test chamber by a fan mounted two-thirds along the duct length. A new Göttingen-type tunnel was commissioned by Nissan in 1985

When all these variations in tunnel design are considered, it is easy to appreciate why individual tunnels can give individual results on the same identical car. For a start, the blockage ratios (cross-sectional area of the tunnel nozzle divided by the cross-sectional area of the test vehicle) vary from 41 to as low as 2, even before the boundary effects of the walls are taken into account. Then there is the contraction ratio of the nozzle (fan area divided by nozzle area), which varies from 9 to 4 and has a significant effect on the stability of the flow. To put some dimensions on the delicacies of achieving a stable tunnel air flow, one of the latest tunnels to be built, commissioned in January 1984 by Ford of Germany in Cologne, took almost nine months to calibrate after construction was completed. As the latest state of the wind-tunnel art, it forms a useful case study which explains the functioning and accuracy standards in use today. It is unusual, if not unique, in having a removable nozzle insert that allows scale models to be tested in the same facility as full-size cars.

In layout the Ford tunnel is a closed-circuit, single return design of the Göttingen type with an open test section configuration. The majority of the shell is constructed in reinforced concrete, with welded steel boiler plates for the contraction duct, fan housing, corner vanes, fan transition parts and collector/ diffuser sections. It uses an electrically-driven single-stage 12-blade fan with 21 ft diameter and variable blade pitch to control air speed.

Each of the four corners contains steel deflector vanes to direct the air uniformly through the turns and there are seven stator blades directly after the fan to prevent flow rotation. There is a semi-ellipsoidal nose cone at the inlet to the fan and a cubic arc tail cone at the outlet. The rotational speed of the fan is fixed at 371 rpm, with open-loop wind speed control through the adjustable blade pitch. This system was chosen because it was cheaper than a variable fan speed and provided better dynamic behaviour of speed variations. Air speed acceleration from 0 to 186 mph can be achieved in only 20 seconds, which speeds up the test sequence time and improves operating efficiencies.

Drive for the motor absorbs 2000 kW (2680 bhp) at 600 volts continuously, with a short duration overload capacity of 30 per cent. With normal outside air temperatures it was calculated that the tunnel air temperature would remain within reasonable limits without an air path heat exchanger, although manually-operated air exchange flaps are provided in the first and second cross legs to accommodate protracted maximum speed test requirements.

For full-scale testing a nozzle measuring 13 ft high by 20 ft wide is provided. With an allowance for small corner fillets, this gives a nozzle area of 256 sq. ft. In European terms, this puts the size of the new Ford tunnel about mid-way between those of Pininfarina (126 sq. ft) and Daimler-Benz (350 sq. ft) and close to the sizes chosen by BMW (215 sq. ft) and Nissan for their very similar new tunnel (298 sq. ft), commissioned in September 1985.

The open test chamber, which has a cross-sectional area 18.6 per cent larger than the nozzle exit, ensures typical open jet characteristics without interference from the test section walls. From the nozzle to the collector inlet the chamber measures 34 ft, which allows a removable insert to be introduced that maintains a stable flow. This insert increases the maximum air speed from 112 mph to 186 mph for scale model testing by increasing the contraction ratio from 4 to 11:1. It has a nozzle area of 93 sq. ft, a test section length of 20 ft and a matching collector insert for the upstream flow.

Very close accuracy limits were set for the stability of air flow, which was

ABOVE RIGHT This is the aerodynamicist's view of a typical wind tunnel control room, with computerized console and soundproof observation window for the test chamber. Hand-held smoke wands are being used here to visualize the flow characteristics on a Ford Sierra XR4i

RIGHT The Ford Cologne tunnel has a movable nozzle and false floor to allow scale model testing in the same facility as full-size cars. A touch-sensitive computer-controlled probe is scanning the model here to record surface coordinates

required to be vertical to within 0.1 degrees and horizontal to within 0.5 degrees. Dynamic pressure deviation is within $\pm$ 1.0 per cent and the axial static pressure gradient within $\pm$ 0.2 per cent of the dynamic mean pressure.

Vertical forces are measured by a hydrostatic seven-component strain gauge balance with an electromechanical tare system. It is installed under the test chamber floor on a separate foundation and mounted on a turntable which allows yaw angles to be induced. Full-sized test vehicles or mock-ups are positioned on four single wheel pads, linked by a lever-arm system to seven precision strain-gauge load cells with a vehicle weight range from 100 to 9000 lb. Accuracy for X, Y and Z components is better than 0.03 per cent.

The turntable can be set at between −100 and +250 degrees from the in-line position, within a tolerance of less than 0.1 degrees. A dedicated 128 kB microcomputer processes the data acquisition and evaluation of results. It provides a simultaneous direct read-out of aerodynamic coefficients and test conditions during running, as well as graphical plotting of collective data and storage of pressure distribution readings from up to 256 pneumatic tappings.

After extensive development of the flow angularity and dynamic pressure distribution in the new Ford tunnel, correlation tests on a special calibration vehicle in four other European facilities (at Daimler-Benz, Fiat, Volkswagen and DNW) confirmed a maximum deviation on drag coefficient of ±0.002, equivalent to an accuracy level of ±0.67 per cent.

The General Motors wind tunnel, the largest dedicated to automotive work in the world, was built at the Warren Technical Center, Michigan, in 1980. It is a similar Göttingen closed-circuit, single-return design, with a much larger test section that measures 18 ft high, 34 ft wide and 70 ft long. It uses a closed chamber and is large enough to take a full-size truck. Maximum air flow speed is 155 mph with a nozzle contraction ratio of 5:1, and it is driven by a variable-speed DC electric six-blade fan absorbing 2984 kW (4000 bhp) at 690 volts. Air flow temperature is controlled by a water/air heat exchanger.

Unlike the variable-pitch aluminium blades of the Ford tunnel fan, those at General Motors are of fixed pitch and made from laminated spruce wood. Acceleration of the air flow is slower, taking 22 seconds to reach 50 mph from rest. The total flow path through the circuit is 978 ft and the walls of the test chamber diverge slightly at 0.24 degrees per side to maintain constant static pressure with boundary layer growth across the closed section.

The six-component, virtual-centre weigh-beam mechanical balance uses electric strain gauges with remote control of the initial calibration. It can accept loads up to 8000 lb and be rotated up to 182 degrees in either direction for yaw tests. Each of the wheel support pads is mounted on its own eccentric turntable to adjust for track and wheelbase differences and each tyre sits on an adjustable riser, matched to the tyre footprint to minimize aerodynamic loads on the wheel support surfaces.

Data acquisition, processing and display/output functions are performed by a fully-dedicated 256 kB computer system located in the control room. It handles 32 channels of analogue data, 14 channels of digital and 10 channels of pulse data input. Due to the unsteady behaviour of aerodynamic forces developed on car shapes, all data is time-averaged with mechanical balance readings being sampled simultaneously 100 times/sec. for 30 seconds before accumulated signals are fed to the computer through an analogue/digital converter. After processing into engineering units, results are fed to several monitors, printers and a pen plotter and stored by transfer to floppy disc.

Less than half the General Motors' diameter (see illustration p. 69), the Ford tunnel fan is made of aluminium and has variable-pitch blades running at constant speed. It can accelerate the air flow from rest to 186 mph in only 20 seconds

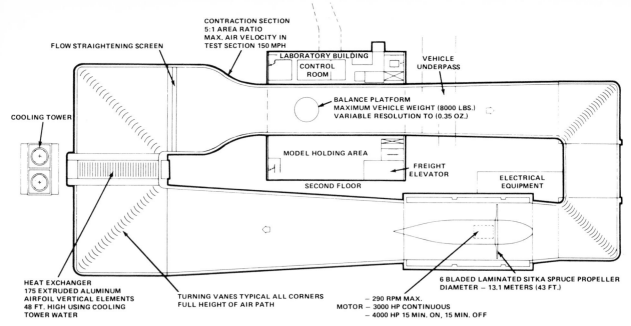

CONTRACTION SECTION
5:1 AREA RATIO
MAX. AIR VELOCITY IN
TEST SECTION 150 MPH

FLOW STRAIGHTENING SCREEN

LABORATORY BUILDING
CONTROL ROOM

VEHICLE UNDERPASS

BALANCE PLATFORM
MAXIMUM VEHICLE WEIGHT (8000 LBS.)
VARIABLE RESOLUTION TO (0.35 OZ.)

COOLING TOWER

MODEL HOLDING AREA

FREIGHT ELEVATOR

ELECTRICAL EQUIPMENT

SECOND FLOOR

HEAT EXCHANGER
175 EXTRUDED ALUMINUM
AIRFOIL VERTICAL ELEMENTS
48 FT. HIGH USING COOLING
TOWER WATER

TURNING VANES TYPICAL ALL CORNERS
FULL HEIGHT OF AIR PATH

— 290 RPM MAX.
MOTOR — 3000 HP CONTINUOUS
— 4000 HP 15 MIN. ON, 15 MIN. OFF

6 BLADED LAMINATED SITKA SPRUCE PROPELLER
DIAMETER — 13.1 METERS (43 FT.)

The General Motors tunnel is used for full-size and scale model testing. When reduced scale models are tested, air flow rates must be increased by the scale factor, which is why these dual-purpose tunnels have such apparently high speed capabilities. A one-third model being tested at 50 mph, for example, requires an air flow to be generated at 150 mph because of what is known as the 'Reynolds' effect' (see Chapter 2).

The Volkswagen wind tunnel at Wolfsburg was completed in 1966 and was a pioneer installation of the closed-circuit semi open-chamber type. It has a nozzle outlet measuring 16 ft high by 25 ft wide, with a contraction ratio of only 4:1. Maximum air speed of 112 mph is provided by a 10-blade variable-pitch constant-speed fan, 33 ft in diameter. As well as being an aerodynamic tunnel, the Wolfsburg installation has a movable test chamber cover which can be drawn across to provide a closed environment for climatic testing between –30 and +45 degrees Celsius under controlled humidity. There is also an underfloor chassis dynamometer for running vehicles under load.

At the other end of the wind tunnel scale, and typical of the less ambitious installations quite common for research and development purposes, Specialised Mouldings Ltd, leading suppliers to the UK-based motor racing industry, built a scale-model tunnel at Huntingdon in 1971. It was an open-circuit, closed-section Eiffel type, with test chamber measuring 5 ft by 4 ft and a maximum air flow speed of 85 mph, provided by a 6-blade 8 ft-diameter fan driven by a 1.7-litre petrol engine. It was originally used for developing vehicle and municipal aerodynamics on applications ranging from cars, trains, boats and hovercraft to tall buildings, chimneys and bridges. When ground effects became so vital to Formula 1 racing car design, in the late 1970s, it was bought by Williams Grand Prix Engineering Ltd and moved to a new location at the team's headquarters in Oxfordshire.

Because it was intended particularly for research into racing car ground effects, special provision was made to eliminate the boundary layer on the floor by a suction slot just ahead of the model test section, a feature also incorporated in the full-scale General Motors tunnel, but not generally included in automotive installations.

ABOVE General Motors' wind tunnel in Detroit is the largest automotive facility in the world and of a similar closed-circuit design to the Volkswagen one. It was only completed in 1980

The sheer scale of the General Motors' fan blades, some 43 ft in diameter, is made clear here by the diminutive size of the two test engineers. It runs at variable speed with fixed-pitch wooden blades

Moving ground simulation

Ground effects on aeroplanes have been studied from as early as 1915, when Alexandre Gustav Eiffel tried unsuccessfully to simulate relative ground movement in a wind tunnel using an endless belt. There are mixed views among auto aerodynamicists, however, on the value and significance of moving floors in wind tunnel testing, although for real 'ground effect' design they must surely be considered essential.

Aerodynamic testing of car bodies in the wind tunnel has long been plagued by the problems of correctly simulating the moving ground. As a vehicle travels over the road in real life, both the air and the road are stationary together and thus no boundary layer exists on the road surface. In a wind tunnel the air moves relative to the ground and a boundary layer is formed.

In setting up a car for test in a wind tunnel there are six different ways of installing the model. It can be freely suspended away from the floor (the method used by Jaray), or it can stand on the ground, which represents the road. It can be mounted on a false floor plate standing clear of the ground, which can be fixed, moving as an endless belt or fitted with suction or blowing ducts to eliminate the boundary layer. It can also be mounted wheel-to-wheel with an identical model of opposite symmetry—known as the 'mirror image' method.

Different investigators over the years have used each of these methods, with considerable variations in the aerodynamic coefficients recorded. For simplicity reasons, fixed ground installations have become the industry standard, with little effect on the comparative results needed for vehicle development. The creation of a ground-plane boundary layer by a fixed floor reduces the drag coefficient by up to 5 per cent, but it also moves the aerodynamic centre upwards, creating tail-end lift and more induced drag from the attitude change in the vehicle's trim.

Most automobile tunnels used for testing full-size cars with relatively high ground clearance ignore this effect, while scale-model tunnels usually need to take it into account because of the reduced proximity of the car to the floor. As a simpler alternative to a moving belt, boundary layer suction slots at the front of the vehicle can be used, as can an injection of high velocity air tangentially to the wall, or the installation of slim deflector fillets at floor level. Pressure distribution measurements carried out by Volkswagen in 1975 across the boundary layer under a full-size car in road tests and in the tunnel showed a very close correlation (1 mph) between recorded maximum speed on the road and the predicted top speed based on fixed-floor tunnel tests.

Early aeronautical researchers looked for easier ways of investigating ground effects, including Elliot Reid of Stanford University, who measured the difference in lift between a biplane in flight close to the ground and in free air in 1929 and Wetmore and Turner who, in 1940, towed a glider behind a car. Its rear bodywork was specially modified to minimize its effect on the aircraft being investigated.

The first successful moving floor to be installed was by Klemin in 1934 in the wind tunnel at New York University. It ran at speeds up to 70 mph and it took four months of development to get it working smoothly without flapping or crowning. It was followed by several other moving floor installations, including one at the US National Aeronautics and Space Administration (NASA) Langley Research Centre, another at the Royal Aeronautical Establishment, Farnborough, and one at the Preston Division of the British Aircraft Corporation, Wharton.

At Imperial College, London, a moving floor was first installed in 1968 to

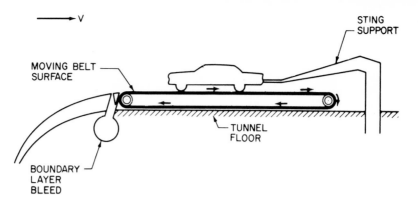

In a typical moving floor tunnel, an endless belt runs at speeds synchronized to the air flow, with a boundary-layer bleed slot at the leading edge of the moving section. The model is supported by a sting bracket and lift forces are measured by strain gauges mounted above

investigate the aerodynamic characteristics of aircraft wings when flying close to the ground. It is now used extensively for racing car development and was supplemented by a newer and larger version, first commissioned late in 1985.

What happens to an aircraft wing as it approaches the ground is something which may well have contributed to several major motor racing accidents. As the ground is approached there is a sudden and appreciable increase in lift. In making a landing in a low-winged aircraft, the pilot counters this to maintain his descent by lifting the nose to change the angle of incidence on the wings, increase drag and provoke stall conditions. Otherwise the aircraft might quite naturally continue flying without actually touching down.

Lift is also increased by the relative movement of the ground interfering with the air flow over the lower surface of the wing section. Under test conditions the difference between a fixed floor and a moving floor amounts to as much as 25 to 30 per cent in lift, depending on the installation, the height of the wing above the floor and its angle of attack.

5 Air flow and the modern car

The starting point for all car design is a set of 'hardpoints' that identify the fixed parameters around which the bodywork envelope must be formed. Each new model is planned to fill a chosen market niche in some way or other, usually as a competitor in a segment already well defined and established. Dimensions such as wheelbase and length are therefore a primary part of the overall package consideration, as is the mechanical layout of the major components. The amount of passenger accommodation and the wheel size are more flexible. The shape of the panels and the amount of glass provided are free in styling terms but constrained in their design by the investment available and manufacturing feasibility.

Each major component takes up a fixed amount of space and its position in relation to the others cannot usually be varied by very much. The mechanical arrangement therefore has a strong influence on how the final car will look and on how much freedom the aerodynamicist will have on the efficiency of the final shape. Having said that, it cannot be overemphasized that there is usually far more to be gained from development of the execution of an existing design than from choosing a potentially low drag initial shape, although certain fundamentals are essential for low drag. What prevents really low drag cars from reaching production in most cases is the cost of the precision and features required, not the inspiration on the drawing board.

No mechanical influence is more significant than the drive arrangement to the wheels, which dictates all manner of other factors such as the footwell room available, installed engine height and even the acceptable length of front overhang.

The pattern of total shape envelopes which emerged in the formative period of car design between the two world wars encouraged the use of long bonnets to symbolize power. At the same time the coachbuilding practice of constructing bodies from a flat platform on top of a separate chassis frame for the running gear left plenty of room for primitive cart suspension and large artillery wheels (a technique derived from the railway carriage-building industry).

In the beginning of motoring the first cars quite often tucked their modest-sized engines out of the way under the rear seats, but as engines became larger and more powerful they moved up to a position at the front traditionally occupied by the horse. And right through to the 1960s, when a new era dawned in mechanical design, the position of the engine varied considerably between the front and the rear in cars of all types and sizes. In the late 1950s, for example, before the front-wheel drive revolution in small cars had taken place, most of Europe was committed to rear engines as fitted to popular cars like the Renault 750/R8/R10, Volkswagen Beetle/1500/411 and Fiat 500/600/850 models.

The influence of drive layout

In terms of vehicle aerodynamics, engine position and the associated drive layout of the vehicle exerts one of the strongest influences on the design. There had always been different ways of driving the wheels since the earliest carriages first went horseless, with little regard for dynamic principles. Although the inherent handling problems associated with the rear weight bias of rear engines produced some very unstable cars at various times in history, it was the complication of steered driving wheels that forced front-wheel drive into the background for many years.

For the rear-mounted engine to have its greatest influence on shape, it needs to dispense with the front radiator and the high flow field pressures of the front compartment (see Chapters 6 and 7) for more information on engine bay air flow

From the initial hardpoints of the mechanical layout a full-size outline is drawn first so that various details of the shape envelope can be developed, using removable plastic overlays and tape lines

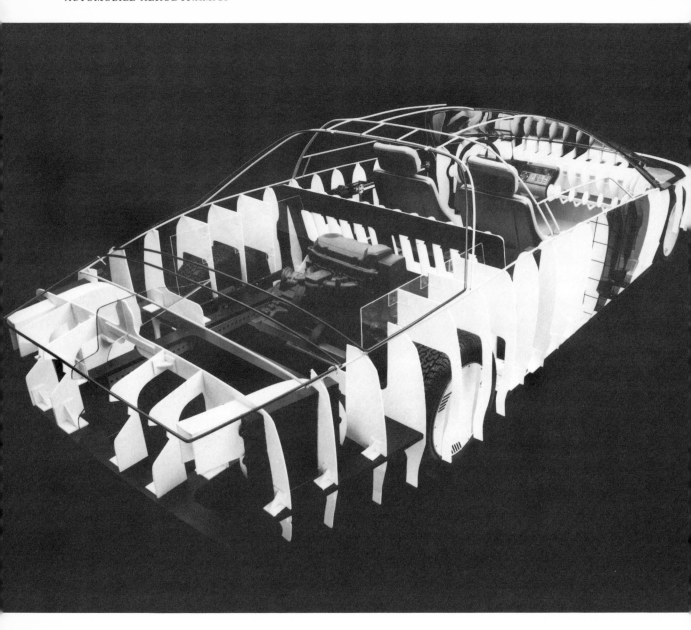

characteristics). The low drag coefficients of the VW Beetle, the closely related Porsche models (and even the extraordinary 1922 Rumpler) and most other rear-drive cars were largely due to their rear mounted cooling systems. Ford developed this concept with a front-mounted engine in the experimental Probe IV design exercise as recently as 1984, installing radiators for engine and air conditioning in the tail with some encouraging drag reductions (see Chapter 9).

But apart from a few specialist sports coupés, influenced more by contemporary racing car design than idealized aerodynamic concepts, the mainstream of the current industry trend is locked into front engines and, for the bulk of the market, front-wheel drive. This fact sets many of the hardpoint limits, like the toeboard and rear seatback positions relative to the suspension and wheelhousings, and usually allows the overall length to be less for the same amount of interior room.

Some of the length reduction is gained by shortening the front overhang,

To allow parallel modelling of interior and exterior features, an interior 'buck' is often used while the exterior clay is being sculptured by the clay modellers. The buck (above) is for the Ford experimental Probe V and the clay (above right) is for the 1976 Fiesta

although the provision of adequate crash protection in frontal impacts and the need to provide a gently sloping nose for good air penetration may work against a short front-end length. With a longitudinally mounted engine arrangement, front-wheel drive often makes less of a length saving than expected (and in the case of the current Audi range, where the engine overhangs the front wheels, length is actually increased).

In aerodynamic terms, the relationship between drive layout and the achievable drag coefficient may not be obvious, given a clean sheet approach to the design. It is certainly possible to develop a very low drag shape with front-wheel drive, as Audi has more than proved with the 100/200/5000 range. But as total drag is the mathematical product of Cd and frontal area (see Chapter 2), rear wheel drive can make the engineering task much easier.

Engine length is a more critical factor in developing low drag than engine height.

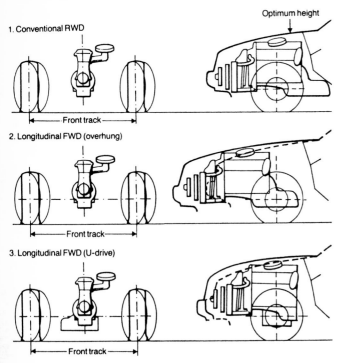

1. Conventional RWD

Optimum height

Front track

2. Longitudinal FWD (overhung)

Front track

3. Longitudinal FWD (U-drive)

Front track

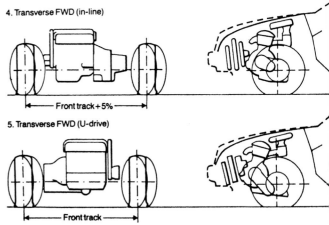

4. Transverse FWD (in-line)

Front track + 5%

5. Transverse FWD (U-drive)

Front track

The shape envelope over the nose of a car is significantly affected by the mechanical layout of the drivetrain components, as is the width of the front track. The installation is further complicated when several engine families must be accommodated in the same design

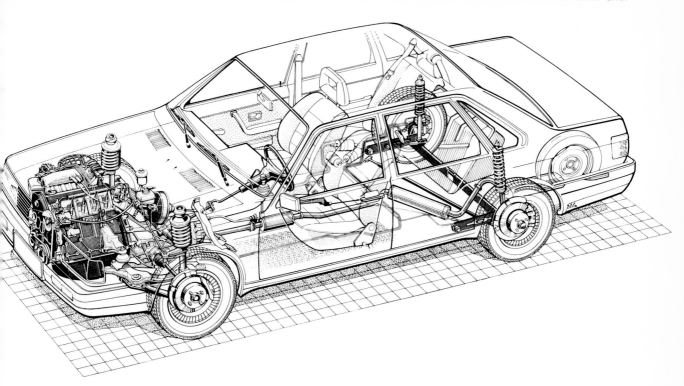

Height is only of secondary importance as cylinders can quite easily be inclined to the vertical to lower the overall power unit package, although such action is more difficult in transverse installations. Manufacturers such as BMW, who incline their longitudinal engines by 30 degrees to the vertical, would introduce severe packaging problems if they tried the same installation with a transverse front-drive design—tilting it rearwards would foul the engine bulkhead and tilting it forwards might foul the bonnet lid where it sloped towards a low nose.

The length of the engine governs the bonnet height at the front when mounted longitudinally and pushes the front suspension strut housings out to make a wider car when mounted transversely. Both these effects increase total drag, either by raising the bonnet lid or increasing frontal area. As little as 3 in. extra body width has been shown to add about 5 per cent to the total drag of a typical modern car, equivalent to increasing the Cd value from 0.38 to 0.40.

It is therefore easier to design a low drag car with a large engine if the power unit can be mounted in line between the front wheels and as low as possible. Where a model line is required to accept a range of engine families (engines for the Ford Sierra, for example, span three different designs from 1.3 to 2.8 litres), the worse case sets the package requirements. This is one of the reasons for the recent rise in popularity of the turbocharger, a device which increases the effective engine power without adding to the physical dimensions of the engine block. It is also the reason why Audi and Mercedes-Benz chose unconventional 5-cylinder engines, instead of more logical and better balanced sixes.

Most of the length saving achieved with front-wheel drive is between the pedal cluster and the rear bumper. This is because the reduced size of the central tunnel, which need only cover the exhaust pipe, brake lines and handbrake cables, allows the pedals to be offset and moved forward. There is no bellhousing between the engine and transmission in the critical footwell area. Front wheelarches intrude

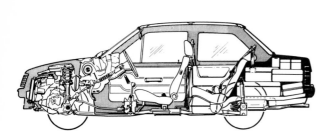

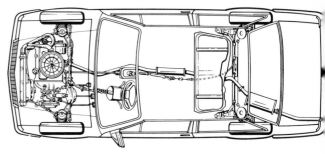

more, however, pushing the pedals over towards the centre of the car and often producing a noticeable offset in the driving position.

The rear of the floor pan under the seat, which would otherwise be swept up to clear the final drive unit, now becomes available for the fuel tank and/or the spare wheel. The suspension location required for a non-driven rear axle can be more easily arranged into a compact, space saving design as well. Length and rear overhang can therefore be saved without reducing luggage compartment volume, although this action has led to the square-backed shapes of small front drive cars which pull larger wake areas behind them and therefore generally have higher Cd values.

On average, front drive cars are about 12 in. shorter than equivalent rear drive models, saving structural weight in the body with significant knock-on benefits through smaller suspension components, brakes, wheels and tyres. On the other hand, rear drive cars that are not required to pass the transmission shafts out to the front wheels can attach the lower ends of their front struts below the hub centres, rather than above or behind them, for better suspension geometry and a lower top housing position.

The regrouping of components at the front in a front drive design increases the proportion of weight at this end from about 52 per cent in the driver-only condition to about 62 per cent, which adds to the steering effort required and makes it more difficult to provide adequate wheel travel for a smooth ride under all loading conditions. Stability is enhanced, however, as the centre of gravity naturally moves further forward relative to the centre of aerodynamic pressure, increasing the 'weathercock' effect at high speed.

Low drag body shapes are not prohibited by the adoption of front-wheel drive, but their development demands far more painstaking attention to small details, such as cooling air flow, bonnet and headlamp sealing, panel joint radii and greater control of production tolerances for consistent manufacturing results.

The elements of low drag design

To the aerodynamic theorist, the starting point for development should always be the ideal shape for a non-turbulent air flow as far as it can be arranged to fit the package hardpoints. This shape would have the minimum projected frontal area for the seating arrangement, the best planform and profile for low drag and as much length as it takes to maintain laminar air flow to a rear point as near the bumper level as possible, for the minimum wake area. In free flight, away from ground influences and the complexities of rotating wheels, a form based on the classic teardrop is the most efficient.

Many researchers through the years have made attempts to combine these ideals

ABOVE *Typical modern small-car package efficiency is shown on these layouts of the Vauxhall Nova (Opel Corsa in Europe). Positioning of the fuel tank under the rear seat and the engine location ahead of the toeboard reduce the overall length by up to 12 in.*

TOP RIGHT *These diagrams highlight some of the key factors that influence the drag coefficient of a modern car, including the front and rear end angles, pillar radii and underbody features*

CENTRE AND BOTTOM RIGHT *During the optimization of a basic car shape the smooth idealized profile (above) must be converted to a more representative scale model form (below). Only then are full-size clays produced for further development*

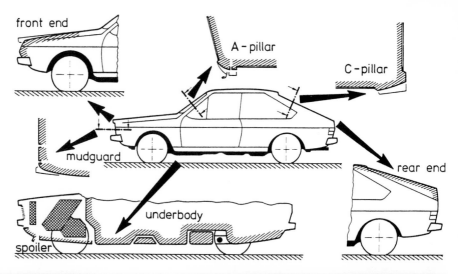

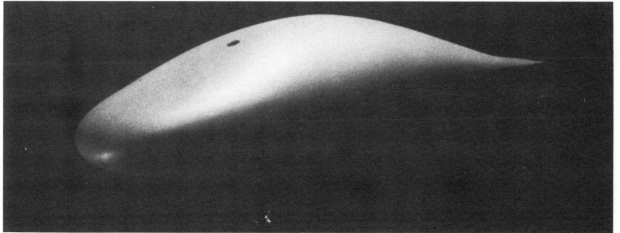

with the functional requirements of motor vehicles, which through the early part of this century at least, averaged between 15 and 20 times less effective than the teardrop in managing their air flow efficiently. Although they could not approach the 0.045 Cd value of a circular section teardrop, drag coefficients comfortably under 0.20 have been achieved for fully operational wheeled shapes, even if the length/height ratios, windscreen rake angles and wheel shrouding required have been undesirable in practical terms.

Basic Criteria for Optimum Aerodynamic Performance

Coefficient	Features Required
Drag (Cd)	Low, well-rounded front end; smooth, rounded junctions between windscreen, A-pillar and body sides; smooth underbody; fastback or squareback rear end.
Side force (Cs)	Well-raked rear window, preferably in full fastback; well-rounded A-pillars and C-pillars; short low bonnet with square lower leading edge; well rounded front and rear wing lines.
Yaw moment (Cy)	As for Cs at front; rear-biased greenhouse position, with rounded edges to roof, fairly upright windscreen and rear window; squared C-pillars and rear wing edges.
Lift (Cl)	Short, low bonnet with squared lower leading edge; smooth underbody, upswept at rear; fairly upright rear window and horizontal boot lid with squared trailing edge.
Pitching moment (Cp)	As for Cl at front; rear-biased greenhouse position, with well-raked rear window; sloping boot lid with rounded trailing edge; square lower trailing edge.
Roll moment (Cr)	As for Cs.

Britain's Motor Industry Research Association based at Nuneaton, Warwickshire, undertook some valuable research into the aerodynamic characteristics of basic forms in the late 1960s, which looked at three fundamental aspects: simple cuboids, saloon car bodies and streamlined shapes. The results showed that the addition of a representative underbody, wheels and wheelarches each contributed approximately equally to a rise in drag coefficient from 0.25 for a plain round-edged cuboid to a Cd value of 0.38. More importantly, a set of basic criteria for each aspect of aerodynamic performance was deduced which formed a basis for aerodynamic development for several years after.

What the MIRA tests highlighted was the need for compromise in aerodynamic design, with each of the several different coefficients demanding totally opposed body features in many cases. A sloping fastback body shape chosen for low drag and a low pitch moment coefficient, for example, was in conflict with the upright rear window angle required for a low lift coefficient and a low yaw moment.

Extending this dichotomy further, low drag body shapes tend to generate high lift forces and high yaw instabilities.

Another significant effort in low drag research was undertaken by the Pininfarina design studios in 1975, working with Professor Alberto Morelli of the Turin Polytechnic, who had already gained considerable experience (and worldwide recognition) in the field of automotive aerodynamics. The fruits of their combined researches produced the now famous Pininfarina 'Banana' car as an idealized shape measured as a full size model in the wind tunnel to record a Cd value of between 0.16 and 0.17.

The way this was achieved was to consider the total body from first principles and deal with its composite drag forces as elements. Each of three drag-generating aspects—form drag, induced drag and skin friction drag—was then dealt with separately to create minimum values. Skin friction was judged to be negligible at all practical vehicle speeds (of the order of 0.03 Cd) and consequently ignored, although it was felt that a minimum 'wetted area' (or a minimum surface/volume ratio) was desirable. To eliminate induced drag, zero aerodynamic lift was essential combined with a zero aerodynamic pitching moment. To minimize the profile or form drag, the area and shape change of the transverse body section were varied as gradually as possible.

Within these objectives a basic body shape was developed, meeting the overall dimensional requirements of a production model and able to accommodate full-size occupants, luggage and powertrain components. This shape, however, did not include suspension and wheel details in its initial form, protuberances for them being added at a later stage. It featured a planform that has since become a critical feature of production low-drag cars, with a tapered front and rear along the general lines of a genuine teardrop, but with the extremities abruptly cut off to contain the overall length and allow a radiator intake to be provided for.

The efficiency of the basic non-wheeled shape was remarkably high, with a Cd value of only 0.071. Adding the wheels and wheelhousings increased this to 0.177 and the lift coefficient from −0.044 to +0.166. Adding an engine cooling inlet was expected to increase the Cd value to 0.187, while cooling air outlets under the car would decrease the induced drag by 20 per cent and reduce the Cd to about 0.165. With a shorter tail, window details and a fully representative underbody, a final value of 0.23 was estimated.

Optimization of body details

Because of the way the motor industry is organized, however, the involvement of the aerodynamicist in a new model design may not start until the final shape has been frozen by company management, although modern computer simulations of the airflow pattern are becoming increasingly effective in determining the initial shapes required for low drag. Approved clay models in general, though, are still based on design proposals from the styling department with input from market research and awareness of competitive trends. In many parts of the motor industry the emphasis has changed recently, however, with the very first clay models now being wind tunnel tested, if not actually tunnel developed to the optimum.

Once the outer skin appearance is fixed, the aerodynamic improvements possible can only be in the form of detail changes, which must only be executed in such a way that the overall styling does not change significantly. This severely restricts the margin of improvement open to the aerodynamicist, which is why he is increasingly

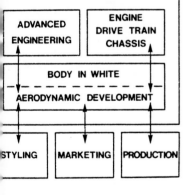

Aerodynamic development has always been an interim development function, positioned between advanced concept studies and styling proposals. There are many interfaces with other company areas, as this Opel organizational chart shows, and a gradual trend towards earlier aerodynamic involvement

becoming involved in the design at the conceptual stage of its development.

In order to set the boundaries of development and establish what degree of drag reduction can be achieved as the ultimate, the first stage in body optimization is to fit a test model with an add-on nose section designed for the best aerodynamic performance regardless of aesthetic or functional considerations. The nose is produced in separate modular sections so that each element can be assessed separately at a later stage. Values of Cd measured against the add-on nose fitted to the model represent the limit against which all practical development can be judged.

In reaching for the ideal, this limit can often be exceeded by other changes to the vehicle, such as a reduction in the angle of the bonnet line, a change to windscreen rake or development of the rear end, but they are excluded from the consideration. This does not necessarily preclude the development of other details, but it separates the work into containable 'packets' as a first stage in the development of the total vehicle. It also allows parallel efforts to be made to reduce lead times if necessary. Under this system designers can develop modular facelifting programmes for existing models at the mid-point of their cycle life using many unchanged panels.

Air dam development must be carried out as part of this front end optimizing process, because even the same spoiler profiles can have very different effects on different front end outlines. In the early stages the optimum aerodynamic nose will usually increase the vehicle length, but with development it can be pushed back progressively without a significant drag penalty to restore the original dimensional hardpoints. The effect of a front air dam is not confined to the shielding of the underbody but often influences the pressure distribution at the rear, where the flow is highly three dimensional and inevitably influenced by the characteristics of the air arriving along the sides and underbody, as well as over the roof. When developing front spoilers, the interference of the tunnel floor is also critical and the thickness of the ground plane boundary layer should not exceed 10 per cent of the vehicle's ground clearance.

Comparative tests on vertical and inclined spoilers have shown no definitive relationship, although when mounted well forward a spoiler's effect on lift corresponds closely to its depth. Both position and depth must be optimized if the best drag and lift reductions are required (see Chapter 7).

The influence of the upper leading edge of the front end (the bonnet lip or upper grille surround) has become a key issue in drag-reducing design. As already explained, the engine length and height affect the panel form at the centre of the car for a longitudinal installation, while bumper and headlamp heights are mostly set by government legislation. Rounding off a leading edge through to the under-bumper apron with an add-on optimized nose extension saves about 10 per cent of the total vehicle drag for a vertical grille, bluff fronted model. Most of this gain, with development, can be achieved by a simple softening of the edge profile radii, or by adoption of the sloping bonnet and low-mounted intake which has become a feature of the latest low-drag body styles.

On vehicles with a short bonnet, this front edge not only influences the drag coefficient but also the pressure in the area just ahead of the windscreen, which in turn controls the ram air available for the heater intake. Generally it is considered desirable to generate enough pressure to give a reasonable heater flow without the need for the booster fan to run continuously, although some new generation cars, like the Audi 100, use a different approach (see Chapter 6).

The position and curvature of the windscreen, and the design of the bodywork ahead of this area, have the most effect on how the air flows around the A-pillars and down the vehicle sides above the waistline. This aspect of aerodynamics is more concerned with wind noise, glass soiling in bad weather and the manufacturing requirements for good fit, although the step level of the A-pillar section and the rebate for the glass mouldings does have a slight effect on drag. It is dealt with in the following chapter, along with other issues classified in industry parlance as environmental air flow.

Although as a general rule the results of front end design optimization can be transferred from one model to a similar one with reasonably close correlation, the same is not true of the rear end. Flow patterns here are determined by both the front-end characteristics and the overall dimensions, and are strongly influenced by the three-dimensional nature of the rear-end design. Notchbacks, fastbacks and estate cars display highly individual wake patterns, often with variable and critical separation points for the twin vortices that trail behind, generating turbulence and drag.

The critical factor in these cases is the angle of the tail from the rear of the roof panel to the rear deck, boot lid or whatever profile the car is designed to meet and which usually contains the rear window. For angles greater than 35 degrees to the horizontal, the point of flow separation is at the rear edge of the roof, generating a trailing wake with a cross-sectional area almost as large as the projected frontal area of the car. The larger the wake area, the more energy it usually takes to pull its turbulence behind the car. For angles less than 30 degrees (the so-called fastback profile), the flow separation moves down to a point much lower and further back, reducing the area of the wake and improving the drag coefficient proportionally.

This transition from slow to fastback angles does not take place suddenly at a specific inclination angle, but in a progressive way across a critical region where the flow separation can easily oscillate up and down the rear window, or break away at different points at different speeds. About 23 degrees rake is the fastback angle at which a coupé provides about the same drag coefficient as a squarebacked estate car, and this is also about the limit of acceptability for rear vision in a production

Flow separation in the form of twin trailing vortices (top left) must be induced to turn inwards for minimum drag. The size of the rear wake is significantly affected by the rear end design and the point of rear flow separation

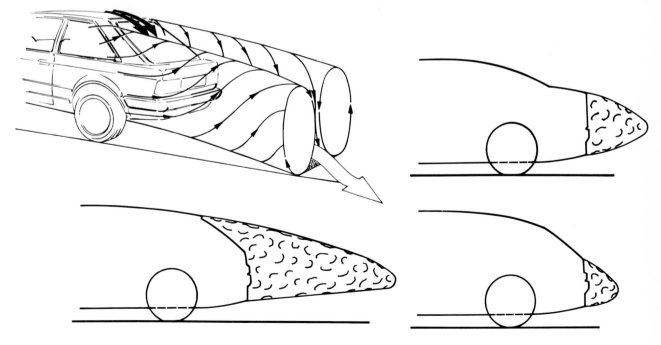

*A major source of drag in all
cars is the wheel and tyre
assembly. Wind-tunnel work
on racing-car tyres, like these
Goodyear tests at Pininfarina,
has been an active part of the
competition scene since the
early sixties*

car. Some more exotic coupés use faster angles, but their buyers are prepared to make greater allowances in return for attention-grabbing style and high performance.

The influence of an add-on rear spoiler at the lower edge of a sloping rear panel is considerable. An optimized rear lip on the 1975 Volkswagen Scirocco, for example, cut the rear lift coefficient by over 33 per cent and at the same time reduced total body drag by about 7 per cent. In reaching the chosen design, six different spoiler profiles were tested in the wind tunnel, with heights ranging from 1.5 to 2.5 in. at three different tail locations, before an intermediate design was chosen.

Small changes in the rear roof contour and C-pillar form can also result in considerable drag reductions or in stability improvements. A horse-collar spoiler around the sides and upper edge of the rear window, for example, as now fitted to several small hatchback saloons, can cut the drag coefficient by almost 10 per cent. On the Ford Sierra some almost undetectable detail changes to the C-pillar plastic mouldings effectively prevented an unstable flow separation at this point in crosswinds without any drag penalty.

Changes of this type do not always produce the expected results. Drag can sometimes be significantly influenced by such small details as the small body gaps between doors or tailgates and bonnet lids. During one set of wind tunnel tests it was found, for example, that the drag coefficient increased by as much as 14 per cent when the upper tailgate edge was sealed to the roof panel and the gap at this point closed off, whereas sealing the side gaps had no effect. The reason for this was determined by smoke visualization techniques, which showed that the separation point moved down to below the rear window when the gap was sealed, generating stronger trailing vortices that absorbed more energy than the less turbulent type from the upper edge.

Wheel and tyre effects

Before 1969 very little was known about the aerodynamic effects of wheels and tyres, apart from the fact that they induced considerable amounts of drag through their bluff forward projected outline and rotational turbulence. Earlier work on aircraft wheels was mostly confined to investigations into ways of generating turning moments to accelerate them before a touch-down.

Working at the Turin Polytechnic, Professor Alberto Morelli studied the behaviour of racing car wheels, both openly mounted as on single-seater racing cars and partially faired-in by the addition of adjustable streamlined covers that could be lowered over the tyres in stages. He did not try to simulate a typical production wheelhousing, although the non-dimensional nature of his results gave his data a degree of aerodynamic validity for all wheel and tyre assemblies.

The test rig, which ran the assembly inverted above the wind tunnel floor on struts, was supported by a conventional six-component strain-gauge balance, with flexibility to apply yaw angles up to 20 degrees, an electric motor to drive the wheel at the same peripheral speed as the airstream and a surface plate into which the tyre was recessed 15 mm to simulate the moving ground and static tyre deflection.

The results showed that a typical rotating bare wheel and tyre had a drag coefficient of between about 0.40 and 0.52 running straight ahead, increasing to over 0.70 at 20 degrees yaw. Fitting smooth wheelcovers to both sides of the rim reduced the Cd by approximately 22 per cent, but adding streamlined 'mudguards' to the upper half contradicted the popular theory that this part of the tyre's rotation

Ford's Probe VI used flexible plastic membranes over the front wheel cutouts to reduce air turbulence along each side of the car, when running straight ahead and with the wheels turned in a corner

was responsible for most of its drag. When the clearance to the tyre tread was reduced below 300 mm, the Cd rose rapidly.

Lift coefficients measured were of the order of 0.2, giving a resultant drag vector angled 25 degrees towards the ground in most of the conditions tested, although these were results which have been disputed by other researchers. As the final phase of his experiments, Professor Morelli tested a 1:4 scale model of a Formula 1 Ferrari, fitted with rotating wheels driven by friction rollers below floor level. This showed that the drag coefficient increased by about 10 per cent when the wheels were turning, while the side force coefficient increased by about 12 per cent almost regardless of yaw angle. More significantly, these tests confirmed that rotating wheels do generate downforce from the differential relative airspeeds on their upper and lower surfaces, which in turn induces about a 10 per cent increase in total drag force at yaw angles below 10 degrees.

6 Cooling air flow and vehicle systems

While the reduction of drag forces and control of lift coefficients are always the primary targets in aerodynamic development work, there are many other factors to be considered. Because they tend to affect the comfort levels of the interior, the operation of the vehicle systems and the driver's overall feeling of control sensed from visibility and stability are generally considered as the important environmental issues relating to the vehicle.

The modern car provides an effective travelling compartment for up to several occupants which is draught-free, quickly warmed when necessary, well ventilated and quiet at high speed. Its interior is protected from uncomfortable pressure variations and the intrusion of dust and exhaust fumes to a remarkable degree. At the same time, the air required to dissipate waste engine heat and cool the brakes is managed scientifically to induce minimum drag without intruding in any way on the interior comfort. These achievements, together with the perceptive safety elements of maintaining clear vision and the active safety elements of providing basic vehicle stability in unstable air flow conditions, are made only through painstaking and meticulous wind tunnel development.

In addition to the aerodynamic wind tunnels already described (see Chapter 4), most manufacturers also have environmental facilities in the form of either another tunnel dedicated to this development work or, like Volkswagen, the ability to convert an existing tunnel for environmental work when required. The key difference between an aerodynamic tunnel and an environmental one is that the ambient conditions can be controlled over a much wider range in the latter and there is usually additional provision for the vehicle to be run under its own power at various loads and speeds on a rolling road or chassis dynamometer while being subjected to air flows.

Control of ambient conditions is arranged through refrigeration equipment (the cooling heat exchanger at Volkswagen's tunnel absorbs 2800 kW) and electric radiant heaters to span a wide range from tropical to arctic temperatures (–22 to +50 degrees Celsius), with relative humidity control up to 95 per cent at +50 degrees Celsius. The working section and the return duct are thermally insulated to prevent heat losses and the formation of ice. These environmental wind tunnels are invariably of the Göttingen recirculatory type, to achieve stable running conditions for each test, although open-circuit Eiffel type tunnels can be used to evaluate deposit patterns by injector spraying of purified chalk water into the air stream.

Test conditions in an environmental tunnel can be selected to represent any kind of typical operation from a cold start-up and driveaway to a simulated solar heat soak with surface temperatures up to the limits found in many desert regions.

Climatic or environmental wind tunnels combine high speed air flow facilities with temperature and humidity control for the testing and development of vehicle systems. At the BL Technology tunnel, a temperature range of between −32 and +55 degrees Celsius is available while cars are driven on a rolling-road chassis dynamometer

Engine warm-up or interior ventilation can therefore be investigated under the controlled and repeatable laboratory conditions essential for effective development.

The pressure distribution along the vehicle centreline section provides an initial evaluation of air resistance and lift characteristics and also enables the systems designer to locate the optimum position for air inlets and outlets for the radiator and engine bay, brakes and passenger compartment. The distribution across the body surface also influences the pressure conditions for the interior, especially at yaw angles other than zero when some pressure zones can actually shift from positive to negative in value, as they can even at zero yaw through body leaks or opened windows.

Heating and ventilation systems

The internal air flow through any vehicle is governed by the available pressures at the inlet and outlet of the total system, the difference being equal to the losses through the system. A differential can be generated by variations of the static pressure around the vehicle while in motion (known as ram air flow), or by a static pressure rise across the blower or booster fan for the heating and ventilation system.

ABOVE *Volkswagen use a sliding cover for the test chamber of their aerodynamic tunnel to control the ambient conditions during climatic tests. This water spray system checks wiper performance and window soiling at high speed*

RIGHT *Flow characteristics along the vehicle centreline can change with road speed if separation bubbles are generated by the shape of the nose panel. Development is usually directed towards maintaining a consistent laminar flow at all speeds*

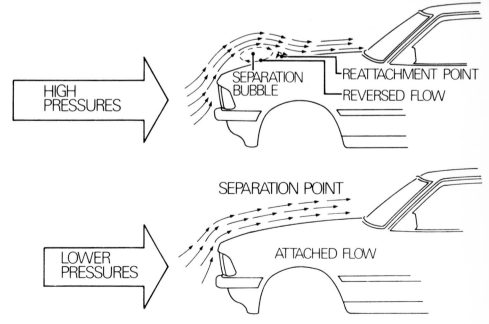

HIGH PRESSURES

SEPARATION BUBBLE

REATTACHMENT POINT

REVERSED FLOW

LOWER PRESSURES

SEPARATION POINT

ATTACHED FLOW

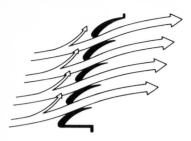

Distribution of air at low speed

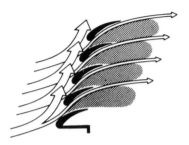

Distribution of air at high speed

Air cushion

Ford used the blocking effect of the air cushion behind louvred airfoil slats in the front grille to match intake cooling air to the engine's requirements without the complication of moving controls

The steeper the windshield angle, the higher the static pressure at its base and the lower the values of the negative pressure profile over the nose of the car, strongly influencing the heater performance

*NACA entry ducts were first developed by the North American aerospace industry as optimized inlets which induced minimum surface drag. They became a feature of many racing cars in the 1960s, being openings flush with the body but venturi-shaped in plan.

To restrict the ingress of dust and fumes, the interior pressure should be slightly above atmospheric but not high enough to cause discomfort by pressure imbalance in the human ear. The flow pattern with windows or sliding roof open must be controlled as far as possible to prevent smells, dust, excessive noise and, particularly, traces of the vehicle's own exhaust being sucked in.

It is therefore highly desirable to locate air inlet openings in areas with positive pressure distribution and in most cars they are positioned at the base of the windscreen where there is most chance of clean, fume-free air being available. The pressure here must be higher than the pressure at the discharge point, wherever that is situated. It increases with the square of the air velocity over the surface and therefore depends on both the speed of the vehicle and the shape of the panels in this area. Factors affecting air pressure at this point include bonnet form, windscreen rake angle and wraparound, booster fan flow and inlet grille design.

The effectiveness of the windscreen in decelerating the air flow over the bonnet and increasing the positive static pressure at the inlet depends to a large degree on the rake angle of the glass. For most conventional saloon shapes, the pressure ratio (static/dynamic pressure) here is between 0.35 and 0.45, decreasing to between 0.1 and 0 at the sides. When windscreens were less curved, the pressure ratio at this point was only 0.15 to 0.20, declining to 0 or 0.1 at the sides. Air inlets for that configuration were therefore usually located at the front behind the radiator grille, although they then tended to draw in more traffic fumes in towns.

Flush surface ducts with a NACA form* provide the highest flow rates with minimum surface drag, but they also show the worst deterioration of flow at yaw angles other than zero. A modern trend towards the installation of wiper arms in slots, to position them out of sight and improve aerodynamics, considerably reduces the pressure at the intake if it is located in the same trough. In some cases negative pressures have been recorded in these slots as little as 10 in. from the vehicle centreline. Cars designed in this way will require their booster fans to be running continuously for the heating and ventilation system to operate effectively.

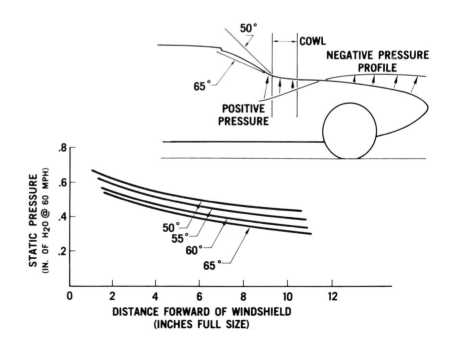

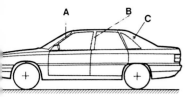

Motor industry convention identifies the roof pillars by letters from the front, ignoring any intermediate support provided by the rear door frames

Since the mid 1960s when Ford pioneered the Aeroflow system, most cars have been fitted with permanent air extractor devices in the form of outlet grilles. At first, to emphasize the customer benefits of positive ventilation, they were made highly visible and usually mounted on the exterior surface of the C-pillar in an area of reasonably low pressure. Later they were incorporated out of sight in the shut flanges of the boot lid or side doors. To be effective, these outlets need to have a total area of at least 16 sq. in., which ensures there is a negative pressure at the outlet while maintaining the interior at close to atmospheric levels.

For a typical saloon notchback with sloping rear window, the pressure distribution ratio on the outer surface of the C-pillar is between −0.4 and −0.8, whereas below the rear window it is only −0.2. When a sliding roof or a side window is slightly opened, the interior pressure distribution ratio drops to −0.6 and air flows in from the outside through all openings. To prevent the car's own exhaust fumes being drawn in under these conditions, one-way rubber flap valves are often fitted out of sight across the extractor ducts below the exterior surface.

Inside the cabin the outlets are usually located at the base of the rear window to induce a demisting flow across its surface, although with the universal fitment of heated backlights many cars now have the outlets in the lower trim pads of the side doors, where the noise of escaping air is less likely to be heard. As warm air from the screen demisting outlets may be obstructed from reaching the side windows, special nozzles are frequently built into the upper ends of the facia capping to direct jets where they can be most effective. The design of these jets and all heater outlets is developed in the environmental wind tunnel to provide slightly stratified interior temperatures which are cooler at face level than in the footwell areas.

Yaw angles of air flow as experienced in crosswinds cause higher negative pressures on the windward side and lower negative pressures on the lee side, but they are balanced in the outlet ducting if this is centrally mounted. Reduced inlet flow rates (20 degrees yaw decreases the flow rate by about 10 per cent) are usually cancelled out by a higher net extraction effect, maintaining fairly uniform cabin pressures.

In modern car design the development of the internal air flow is a complex process, optimized by wind tunnel and road test development. The 1981 Ford Escort used extractor grilles hidden in the side door jambs

TERRY COLLINS

Window soiling

However well a car's tyres may be shrouded, assuming that conventional cutouts are used to allow the front wheels to steer, road dirt will be splashed along the side surface rearwards in the shape of a typical parabolic trajectory with the road surface as its horizontal centreline. Vertical rear surfaces are also subjected to deposits resulting from the backwash of turbulent air that spins off the rear of the bodywork in twin trailing vortices. The size and intensity of this turbulence is determined by the area of the wake induced, itself a function of the point at which the laminar air flow separates from the body surface.

Careful attention to body details can reduce the areas soiled and special gutter mouldings for the A-pillars can prevent water rivulets running round from the windscreen to leave dirty streaks on side windows. The problem of tail panel soiling has never been satisfactorily solved and has in many cases been aggravated by the development of low drag shapes with smaller, more intensive wake areas. In most cases, except those of small hatchbacks or squarebacked estate cars, it is possible to optimize the rear roof contour to keep the rear window from being included in the soiled area.

To alleviate the problem of insect impingement on forward facing surfaces like headlamp lenses and the windscreen, many deflector devices appeared in the early 1950s. They were seldom totally effective, as the inertia of the airborne particles is too great for them to be diverted sufficiently and most insects ended up splattered on the surface of the device. An alternative system developed by Mercedes-Benz using an active 'air curtain' generated by an engine driven blower fan produced more encouraging results, but revealed several major shortcomings when translated from a scale model into a full-size prototype. As well as requiring too much power, its thermal currents created an optical distortion when viewed through the screen which was distracting to drivers.

Some ingenious details were introduced on the Mercedes-Benz S-Class cars in 1979, to prevent window and lamp lens soiling through advanced design and wind tunnel development. Water flowing over the roof at high speed, for example, was fed through rain channels in the rear window surround to a drain trough formed in the joint between the boot lid and the body, avoiding the rear glass. To keep the tail lamps clean and visually effective, the air flow was fed round the lamp cluster from the rear quarter panel and the surfaces of the lenses ribbed to leave half their area free from dirt deposited by the upward swirling vortex each side.

Optimized engine cooling

When the emphasis of car design first turned seriously to the reduction of fuel consumption (see Chapter 8), aerodynamic development of engine cooling systems became a priority objective. Since the earliest days of land speed record breaking, when ice tanks were sometimes used to eliminate radiator air flow completely, the energy required for cooling systems was well known. But reaching the optimum design for production cars was hardly ever considered as part of the initial design, and trial-and-error techniques were the general order of the day.

Most manufacturers turned their attention to the cooling system in the 1970s as a primary drag source in the new fuel-efficient vehicles they were designing. They investigated total cooling requirements and air flow distributions through front grilles and across engine compartments in considerable detail, using all manner of

The latest trend towards low mounted air intakes is aimed primarily at reducing drag by smoothing the air flow over the upper surfaces. Any changes must be properly balanced by development of the internal air flow through the engine compartment

aerodynamic test equipment from revolving-vane anemometers to smoke wands and pressure tappings.

Ford test engineers performed some valuable pioneering work on 1974 models which they tested with a variety of front end configurations, ranging from a completely stripped skeleton structure to the fully-dressed production trim. They measured the losses caused by each body component on the total air flow and the recovery generated by the addition of an air dam, cooling fan and its shroud at 30 and 60 mph.

Speed of test	1974 Ford Pinto 30 mph	60 mph	1974 Ford Mustang 30 mph	60 mph
Total ram air (cu. ft/min.)	1340	3030	1440	3240
Losses				
Bumper	−710	−1210	−770	−973
Grille	−130	−170	−170	−527
Recovery				
Air dam	+530	+950	+435	+845
Fan and shroud	+750	+780	+940	+890
NET TOTAL	+1780	+3380	+1875	+3475
Breakdown				
Ram air	28%	49%	27%	50%
Air dam	30%	28%	23%	24%
Fan and shroud	42%	23%	50%	26%
	100%	100%	100%	100%

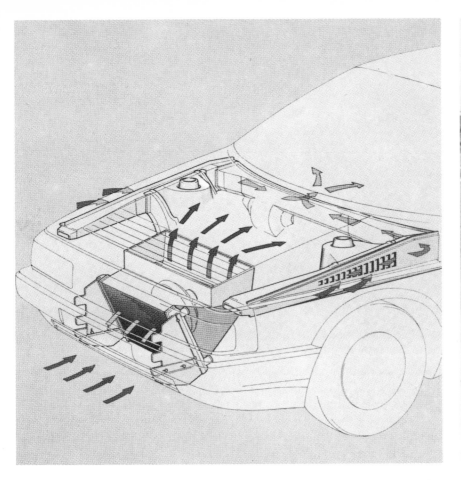

This table alone provides more justification for the widespread introduction of air dams than any other set of test data, showing how a large proportion of the bumper losses (between 50 and 65 per cent) could be recovered. It also shows the value of another trend dating from that time of substituting viscous coupling clutches for fixed mechanical fan drives. As vehicle speed rises, the need for a positive cooling fan flow reduces.

Flow distribution tests undertaken at the same time showed that at 30 mph there was a reversal of the air stream behind the bumper of these square-fronted body shapes which was both inefficient for cooling and highly drag inducing. The solution has been to develop fully ducted cooling systems with lower intake positions, often incorporated into moulded plastic bumpers or located in the under bumper area where there are higher static pressures and less intrusion into the penetrating air stream.

Later wind tunnel tests in 1980, also conducted by Ford, on a wide range of conventional vehicles showed that the intake for the cooling air accounted for between 5 and 15 per cent of the total aerodynamic drag. Research also showed that the normal combination of ram air and fan cooling used 20 per cent more power than the fan moving the same quantity of air alone. So various alternative side-entry systems were investigated, one of which was incorporated in the Probe IV fully functional design exercise, revealed at the Geneva Motor Show in March 1982 (see Chapter 9).

To achieve a low drag unspoiled by the need for a radiator inlet opening at the

ABOVE LEFT *Ducting the cooling air from a low intake to a bonnet-top outlet has been shown to be very efficient on several design studies, like this Volkswagen Auto 2000 developed in 1981. The cost element has so far prevented such systems reaching production*

ABOVE *Aston Martin improved the drag coefficient of their bluff fronted V8 Vantage coupé by sealing off the above-bumper grille and ducting the cooling air through slots underneath*

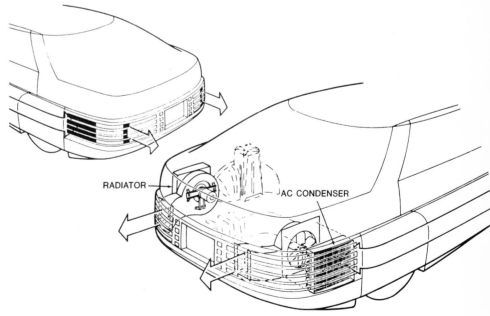

RADIATOR

AC CONDENSER

Cooling air flow was transposed to the rear on the Ford Probe IV design study, with twin radiators drawing their air from side intakes and exhausting through the tail

front, small twin radiators for engine and air conditioning system were mounted each side in the rear quarters in space normally wasted behind the wheelhousings. The heat dissipated through finned connecting pipes and the separation of these two radiators (more normally stacked one behind the other at the front) enabled them to be made considerably smaller than conventional units.

Cooling air was drawn directly to each radiator through an optimized inlet on the bodyside, about 12 in. from each corner, by a special slim radial-flow electric fan. It discharged through outlets in the rear panel about 8 in. inboard, adding to the positive pressure draught generated by a forced ventilation system for the front engine compartment, ducted through the central tunnel containing the exhaust pipes and the finned radiator connecting tubes. It was claimed that the combined system reduced total aerodynamic drag by over 3 per cent to the remarkably low level of 0.152.

Wind noise

Low interior noise has become an increasingly important criterion in modern automotive design, as comfort levels and competitive market pressures have advanced. At high speeds, aerodynamically induced interior noise now constitutes the prime disturbance to be controlled during vehicle development in the wind tunnel and by road testing under real-world conditions. Although the dominating sources in most cases can be localized, eliminating the unsteady flow characteristics over the body surface in the areas affected is one of the hardest aerodynamic tasks.

Over the past decade there has been considerable progress in the insulation and suppression of noise, vibration and harshness (NVH) from mechanical components. Sophisticated vibration analysis using computer models (see Chapter 12) has optimized the structural members and supporting systems to the point where the total mechanical noise level forms only about half the total noise experienced inside the vehicle at normal cruising speeds. For further overall improvements to be made in running refinement, sources of aerodynamically induced interior noise are of prime importance.

Although low drag bodies generally tend to induce less wind noise than higher drag shapes, localized flow separation from small-scale disturbances on the body surface that may not have much influence on the Cd can nonetheless be a major source of interior noise. And the problem usually facing the development engineer when making assessments is either that the wind tunnel itself produces too much background noise, or that road noise during track tests masks sound recordings taken in the cabin.

The best environment for wind noise analysis is the test section of a closed chamber tunnel with a large cross-sectional area. Volkswagen found that the 26 × 20 ft DNW tunnel was appreciably better than their own 25 × 16 ft facility, giving a noise-to-signal ratio of about 10 dB. In their tests a total of seven microphones were installed at ear level, although the most critical position is that corresponding with the driver's outboard ear. As no pronounced acoustic resonances occurred anywhere across the interior, the driver's ear microphone became the controlling factor in subsequent development.

Several different phenomena were investigated in this 1982 study, including the surface pressure characteristics of both fastback and notchback body shapes, the relative importance of different noise contributing sources and the potential available for future noise reduction. The conclusions reached were that road noise

ABOVE RIGHT *Wind noise is measured in climatic wind tunnels by microphones positioned where the driver's ears would normally be. Although low drag usually reduces wind noise, there are many other factors to be developed for a really quiet car*

RIGHT *Disturbed air drumming on the underfloor surfaces can cause interior noise levels to rise, so the next stage in aerodynamic development is being directed towards smooth underbodies like this Ford Probe III proposal*

Flush glass for the side windows as well as front and rear screens was pioneered in the Audi 100, helping it to set new aerodynamic standards which have never been convincingly beaten

was the dominant factor up to speeds of about 90 mph, above which speed it was the body gaps and the resonances in the gap behind them that held the best scope for future improvement. Although screen wipers actually increased wind noise recorded on the exterior by some 6 dB, the low surface pressure existing at the base of the screen meant the effects were negligible at the interior observation point.

The effect of adding door mirrors was totally different. Here the flow deflection they created moved the A-pillar vortex upwards, increasing the side window area exposed to low surface pressures and reducing audible noise. But their turbulent wake then had a more disturbing effect which more than offset the initial improvement, adding between 1 and 2 dB to the interior noise recorded. Moving the mounting position rearwards, as on the 1984 Series 2 Golf, also moves the pressure fluctuation away from the driver's ear, reducing interior noise quite noticeably.

Another major source of aerodynamic noise was found to be caused by aerodynamic pressure fluctuations of the body floor, especially if no attempt has been made to smooth in the many protrusions normally found under a car. During road tests with instrumented cars this effect was even more noticeable, due to the increase in local flow velocities caused by the absence of a ground/floor boundary layer. As well as underbody smoothing to reduce the pressure fluctuations, additional vibrational damping of the floor structure can significantly lower interior noise.

The major potential for aerodynamic noise reduction in the future seems to be indicated by several fields of development which might prove fruitful. One already established by Audi is the use of flush glass to prevent flow separation downstream of window frames and surface sealing of door gaps, as introduced by several manufacturers over the past two years. Optimization of air flow around door-mounted mirrors by the use of extended fairings has so far been hampered by safety legislation requiring knock-back resilience when contacted by pedestrians, although alternative ways of meeting the same intent are being investigated. In the long term it has been predicted with some confidence that against a baseline of 1980/82 standards, noise levels from aerodynamic sources can eventually be reduced by about 10 dB for the average small, family-sized car.

7 Air dams, spoilers, side-skirts and fins

Although ducts, scoops, deflectors and sloping windscreens of various types have been used on cars since the very earliest days of motoring and motor racing, the use of air dams, spoilers and fins dates from the early fifties. Some may have been based on early wind tunnel results in some instances, but these features were quickly degraded into a styling gimmick. Side skirts are more modern, reflecting the era of ground effect racing cars (see Chapter 10), but are far from effective without the integrated underbody design found on competition machines. And between the two extremes of aerodynamic function and styling form, which have only this decade been blended in harmony, came a plethora of devices ranging from bug deflectors to portholes and nacelle-backed mirrors.

Fashion in car styling historically is based as much on image as engineering fact. Extremes like the Cadillac tail fins of the late 1950s were really no more than an almost subliminal reflection of the early jet plane era, and were used to create sales demand in a home market which was in decline. As the strength of the dollar grew overseas, so the traditional US car exports started to dry up, putting more pressure on domestic sales. So each year the industry launched bigger and better new models, designed to be the latest high style and irresistible to the consumer. And they did it by the use of extremes.

In pursuit of the 'Buck Rogers' image, windows began to spread round the cabin sides as the technology for bending glass improved and in 1953 there was a dramatic swing to curved windscreens. At the same time cars became lower and longer, to the point where a supplementary new market opened up for what became known as 'compact' models. To relieve the slab sides of the 'regular' oversize American sedan (that stretched to some 18 ft in length) and add feature interest to other areas of plain painted metal, panels became sculptured and decorated, grilles grew to full width, tail lamps were enlarged and styled into distinctive shapes and chrome plating appeared at every conceivable excuse.

Fins as a styling gimmick were really born in Detroit in the early 1950s, with many designers claiming to be the first in the field. Chrysler's finned models were first launched on the unsuspecting public in 1957, shortly after General Motors had tested public reaction by a series of show cars. They were supported at the time by results obtained using a fully detailed three-eighths scale model, complete with rotating wheels and model cooling fans behind the model radiator, in the University of Detroit's wind tunnel. By comparing the pressure distribution from 100 surface tappings and several hundred wool tufts with and without fins on the same model at extreme yaw angles, it was verified that the stylized tail fins reduced steering corrections in strong crosswinds by up to 20 per cent. Three years later data from

ABOVE *General Motors and Chrysler led the US auto industry into an era of tail fins which lasted from the early 1950s for at least ten years. This experimental Buick Wildcat convertible, first shown in 1955, featured fins, chrome portholes on the bonnet top and vast areas of ornamental chrome*

RIGHT *The first spoiler to appear on a production car was fitted to the Porsche 911 Carrera RS coupé, announced at the end of 1972. By 1973 it had been redesigned to incorporate the soft plastic edge shown here, for improved pedestrian safety*

the same series of tests were used to develop headlamp and windscreen changes that reduced drag by 15 per cent.

In the mid 1960s two English researchers undertook some more extensive tests on the aerodynamic effects of fins. They used a wide range of sizes on the rear end of a contemporary American car of that era in the MIRA wind tunnel at an air speed of 40 mph with up to 25 degrees yaw angle. Triangular and rectangular fin shapes were tried, with surface areas up to 4.152 sq. ft and heights up to 19 in. As might be expected, the triangular fins proved more effective because they protruded further beyond the boundary layer than the rectangular fins and therefore applied more leverage to the car about its yaw centre. All fins were mounted on the boot lid appreciably below the roof line.

Most fins also reduced the drag coefficient slightly, presumably by reducing the tail end turbulence of the wake, but the conclusion reached was that to be effective tail fins needed to be unacceptably large. It was confirmed, however, that small paired triangular fins of the type fitted to many American cars at that time could realistically be claimed to enhance stability by reducing the adverse aerodynamic yawing moments.

Air dams and spoilers

The earliest applications of front underbody air dams and rear deck spoilers appeared as add-on devices on competition cars in the early sixties. Their purpose was to reduce aerodynamic lift coefficients for improved high speed stability and handling. The Ferrari 246 P sports prototype driven by Ricardo Rodriguez in the

1962 Targa Florio was the first design to feature a distinctive rear spoiler, similar to that which appeared the following year on the now classic Ferrari 250 GTO. In 1964, front air dams, in the form of diminutive and separated lower air deflectors, appeared on some versions of the Ferrari 330 P2.

Full width air dams increased cooling flow to the engine and both dams and spoilers often reduced the drag coefficient, but the flow field effects and associated surface pressure changes producing the improvements were not generally understood. All that was known was that front lift reduced the friction forces on the steered wheels causing understeer in high speed corners and that rear lift reduced the tractive effort and could cause high speed wheel slip.

One of the first production cars to promote the application of these aerodynamic aids as highly visible body features was the 1972 Porsche Carrera RS coupé, which was fitted with both a front air dam and a very prominent rear deck spoiler. The following year it was redesigned with a soft plastic surround to add a degree of pedestrian safety to what would otherwise be a sharp fibreglass edge (the scope for more gentle fairing of the device was inhibited by the need for cooling air intakes on the rear-engined design of the 911 model).

The effectiveness of these devices was dramatic. At a speed of 90 mph front lift was reduced by some 90 per cent from about 45 lb to less than 5 lb, while at the rear there was an even greater lift reduction of almost 100 lb. But more important than the lift reductions achieved (and a small decrease in the CdxA value by 2 per cent) was the decrease in the sensitivity to side winds, as shown by the movement of the pressure centre with yaw angle. Here the improvement averaged around 25–30 per cent.

Another test undertaken by Porsche to verify the effect of the dam/spoiler system

By 1957 tail fins had started to grow larger, with much publicity about their aerodynamic advantages in crosswinds at high speed. The credibility of the advertisements was never very strong in design terms

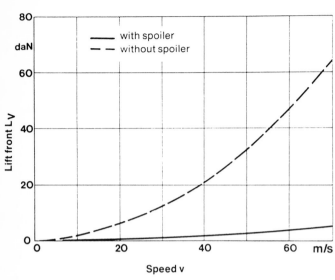

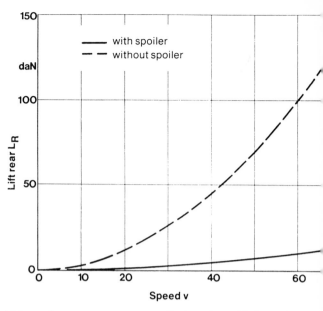

These graphs show the effectiveness of the front and rear spoilers fitted to the 1973 Porsche 911 Carrera RS coupé, which reduced front and rear end lift by about 90 per cent. They started a trend which was widely copied

was a high-speed (120 mph) lane-change manoeuvre applied as sinusoidal steering input. The results showed no change in the initial response (important for a positive feel), but a decrease in both the secondary deflection and the time taken to damp it out.

General Motors undertook a series of dam and spoiler tests on a three-eighths scale semi-detailed model in 1976 to record force and moment measurements of a typical notchback body shape, supplemented by engine compartment and ground plane surface pressure measurements, as well as flow visualization experiments. The results identified the lift and drag contributions of various model components and the changes caused by the addition of dams and spoilers. They also suggested mechanisms for the flow field behaviour which explained the pressure and force changes observed in the tunnel.

The detailing of the model used was fairly intricate, with a fibreglass outer shell built on a wooden underbody and including a fully simulated engine compartment with a radiator restriction (50 per cent solid metal screen), simplified front and rear suspension components as well as floor pan protrusions. Engine compartment flow rates were monitored by two fan-type anemometers mounted behind the simulated radiator, with a strain-gauge balance measuring aerodynamic forces and moments. Pressure tappings were taken from the model and ground plane surfaces, primarily in the plane of model symmetry. All testing was at zero yaw angle.

Investigations into front air dams were based on a plain lip being added under the bumper about 2 ft ahead of the front wheel centre line where the front apron was about 12 in. above the ground. A range of dam depths was tried, from 1 in. down to virtually ground level without the benefit, it should be noted, of a moving floor installation. The 12 in. dam, of course, was well outside the practical limit for a road car, but it allowed the full relationship to be explored with some interesting results.

The trough of the drag coefficient reduction curve, for example, coincided quite well with the practical dam depth limit of 5 in., but the front lift reduction continued to improve almost to ground level, although with an asymptotic tendency. At any given dam height, the front lift component changed by a much larger amount than either the rear lift or the total drag.

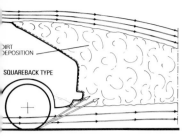

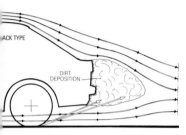

Air flow at the rear of a hatchback shape (above) *is highly critical of the rear window angle, which affects both the size of the rear wake and the dirt deposition pattern on wet roads. Rear spoilers* (below right) *can guide the air flow downwards to a lower separation point, reducing drag at the rear end*

A range of rear spoilers was also tried on the same model, all set at 20 degrees to the vertical across the full tail width and up to 4 in. in height. Here the results were similar to those for a front air dam in regard to aerodynamic drag and lift change reactions at the opposite end of the model, but rear spoilers continued to reduce the rear axle lift component with no apparent limit.

Flow patterns under the car were determined by the use of pressure tappings in the ground plane, because readings taken from the underbody surface were affected too much by the localized disturbances of detail components and floor pan depressions. Comparative tests with a smoothed underbody in the tunnel and correlation tests undertaken 2 in. above the ground on the road proved that ground pressure readings were more representative. The results showed that the largest pressure changes caused by air dams occur between the dam and the front underbody protrusions immediately behind the open-bottomed engine bay, and that the dam effectively diverts the underbody flow away from intrusions like the front crossmember, suspension components and engine projections.

Front air dams also produce a worthwhile decrease in engine compartment interior pressure, which makes a significant contribution to total vehicle drag. Without a front dam, air entering the radiator from under the bumper actually has a partial blocking effect on the main flow and confuses the exit conditions sufficiently to cause a pressure build up in the engine bay. A dam with a depth of only 4 in. was found to increase the cooling air flow by as much as 25 per cent. And an increase in the radiator solidity from 30 to 50 per cent, which further reduces engine compartment pressures, increased total drag by only 1 per cent, but lowered the lift coefficients by an average of 10 per cent.

By the time the air stream over the body surface reaches the rear half of a typical car, it has developed into a highly three-dimensional flow, which eventually develops into a pair of trailing vortices that form the vehicle wake (see Chapter 5). The effect of a rear spoiler depends very much on where the upper surface flow separation takes place and how far into the boundary layer turbulence in this area the spoiler is able to reach. Usually in a notchback design the flow separates at the rear edge of the roof panel where there is the transition from sheet metal to glass

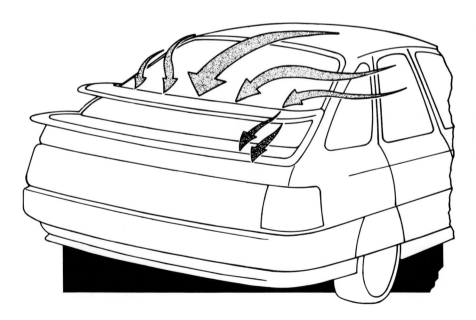

and an acute profile angle change, reattaching again at the edge of the boot lid. In a fastback design, particularly with a steep rake (as on most compact hatchbacks), the flow is unlikely to reattach at all so that a much larger wake area is produced.

The downwash flow in the centre of the rear window adds vertical momentum to the flow at this point, which is usually what initiates the spinning of the wake vortices. Rear spoilers at the trailing edge of the boot lid or hatchback tailgate intercept and divert the downwash, reducing the streamline curvature and increasing the static pressure as far forward as the middle of the roof. This increase reduces the total drag and the lift components, although the pressure drop across the spoiler itself partially negates the net gain which results.

Volkswagen's investigations into front spoilers formed part of a broader study of optimized front-end design. Their researchers found that the angle of a front spoiler made little difference to either drag coefficient or lift, its depth and position being far more critical. In a series of tests on different spoilers with depths from .75 to 2.5 in. at three locations ahead of the front wheels, they were able to achieve up to 15 per cent reduction in Cd and up to 21 per cent reduction in aerodynamic lift.

In a detailed wind tunnel comparison of modifications and add-on equipment available in the after-market, John Miles (then on the technical staff of *Autocar* magazine) tried to improve the drag and lift characteristics of a Ford Capri S. The table shows the results of the changes made, step by step, and makes an interesting comparison with the work quoted in Chapter 11 for a similar-shaped fastback coupé developed for racing.

Conversion of a standard Ford Capri (above) into an aerodynamic special (like the Tickford version, right) is only effective when the add-on devices have been properly developed in a wind tunnel. Using a scientific approach, significant drag and lift reductions are possible

AERODYNAMIC DEVELOPMENT OF FORD CAPRI S

Conditions	Cd	Clf	Clr
Standard car (as tested)	0.414	0.288	0.101
Fit deeper front spoiler	0.409	0.233	0.104
Close bumper-body gap	0.406	0.225	0.104
Smooth wheel trims	0.396	0.225	0.104
Fit larger rear spoiler	0.397	0.230	0.030
Raise rear spoiler (add airfoil)	0.401	0.233	0.089
Fit intermediate rear spoiler	0.383	0.228	0.064
Add lower lip to front spoiler	0.375	0.198	0.071

Body kits tested

In a rather more general testing exercise, *Performance Car* magazine compared wind tunnel measurements on three sets of after-market bodywork kits against a standard Ford Escort XR3i, a car which in standard form is claimed to have the reasonably low drag coefficient of around 0.385. This is partially achieved through factory-developed add-on body parts, such as a front spoiler lower lip merging into front wheel shrouds, moulded rear wheel shrouds and a prominent rear tailgate spoiler.

Working from an initial value of 0.395 for the standard car (each wind tunnel gives a slightly different coefficient and each car may deviate slightly from the production specification in regard to such items as ride height, attitude and sheet metal fit), the three sets of body kits were tested in turn. This was not a controlled

back-to-back test as performed by industry development teams, but an assessment of four different cars that were not necessarily identical in their basic physical properties. Despite this qualification, the results were interesting, particularly as they were conducted at three different yaw angle settings.

The kits were all of similar intent, in that they were meant to dress the Escort up to look like a smart and stylish 'racer' with colour coordinated add-on panels, usually for the front under-bumper spoiler, the door sills in the lower area each side between the wheels and for the rear tailgate. The Kamei equipped car used the standard rear spoiler (itself the result of Ford's own intensive wind tunnel tests), but included a pair of small tapered 'fences' for the crowns of each front wing, intended to prevent air spilling over the sides and generating turbulence. The KAT body kit was tested with two alternative rear spoilers, the Mark II being larger.

The conclusions that can be drawn from this series of tests are varied. For a start, the basic Escort shape was specifically developed to maintain a low drag value under yaw conditions (it deteriorated by only 15 per cent at 20 degrees yaw), probably at the expense of ultimate Cd values. The Kamei and KAT body kits were therefore able to improve on the base car's total drag coefficient.

Dozens of different body kits are available for cars like the Ford Escort shown here and the VW Golf GTi. Their effects are not always beneficial in reducing drag and lift

AERODYNAMIC TESTS ON FORD ESCORT XR3i

Model tested		Cd	Clf	Clr
Standard car	Yaw angle = 0°	0.395	0.151	0.036
	Yaw angle = 10°	0.412	0.242	0.071
	Yaw angle = 20°	0.456	0.375	0.219
Cartel body kit	Yaw angle = 0°	0.407	0.133	0.069
	Yaw angle = 10°	0.436	0.198	0.117
	Yaw angle = 20°	0.478	0.272	0.162
Kamei body kit	Yaw angle = 0°	0.391	0.124	0.120
	Yaw angle = 10°	0.429	0.189	0.126
	Yaw angle = 20°	0.484	0.273	0.203
KAT I body kit	Yaw angle = 0°	0.379	0.113	0.150
	Yaw angle = 10°	0.430	0.174	0.167
	Yaw angle = 20°	0.482	0.303	0.251
KAT II body kit	Yaw angle = 0°	0.380	0.105	0.098
	Yaw angle = 10°	0.433	0.168	0.126
	Yaw angle = 20°	0.482	0.303	0.214

But the lower drag versions were all inferior to the standard car at 20 degrees yaw, proving the point and showing the intricacies of aerodynamics very clearly. On front end lift, all the larger front spoilers did a good job at reducing this component, although the same was not true at the rear. All four kits actually increased rear end lift at zero yaw (straight ahead) and at 10 degrees yaw angle, but mostly reduced the value by different amounts at 20 degrees yaw (the one exception being the KAT I body kit which generated more air pressure under its surface than above, increasing rear lift by 15 per cent at 20 degrees yaw).

Rally cars: function first

As in the field of Formula 1 Grand Prix racing (see Chapter 10), there is little need for low drag considerations on international class rally cars in the ultimate Group B category. As power outputs have increased, it is traction under acceleration and through corners which has dictated the functional needs of cars that do not have the space to reach high absolute speeds. Aerodynamic design has therefore been focused on downforce.

Although the appearance of cars like the MG 6R4 rally car might suggest a desperate need for an aerodynamicist to 'clean up' the exterior skin, which is precisely what the Austin Rover design department has done with the experimental MG EX-E derivative (see Chapter 12), the fact remains that this breed of machine does have considerable aerodynamic design behind it. Within a bodyshell that the public can (just) relate to the production MG Metro selling in the dealerships, it manages the air flow over its 'garden shed' aesthetics to generate cooling flows for engine and brakes combined with considerable levels of aerodynamic downforce.

To improve ground clearance over the rough surfaces of forest stages, the soft plastic air dam is supplemented by a front airfoil, cantilevered forward on dumb-

iron brackets. It forms a slot to deflect air over the nose of the car with a choice of five angles of attack, adjusted by repositioning set-bolts in the selected dumb iron holes.

The rear airfoil, mounted on stub fins each side of the rear window, forms another slot to maintain laminar flow at the separation point and has a similar plain section with four angles of adjustment. As the fast servicing requirements for a rally car prevent much in the way of underbody fairings, the motorsport engineers responsible for the 6R4 design did not feel it necessary to test the model in a tunnel with a moving floor. Development concentrated more on achieving adequate and adjustable front and rear downforces to complement the handling characteristics of the four-wheel drive system.

Other examples of the new-generation Group B four-wheel drive rally cars, such as the Ford RS200 and the Peugeot 205 Turbo 16, feature much smoother skin surfaces than the MG but do not have the same provisions for generating downforce. Undoubtedly the most efficient in drag terms is the Porsche 959.

In competition terms spoilers fall into two categories (see also Chapters 10 and 11). There is the deflector or surface-mounted spoiler designed simply to redirect air flow and redistribute the surface air pressure. And there is the true airfoil, detached from the surface to generate downforce by the same principles as those which make an aircraft wing support weight and fly. Both types add considerably to the total body drag.

Deflectors or spoilers (so called because they 'spoil' the natural flow pattern) are

To be truly effective in generating downforce, front and rear wings must be clear of the bodywork and aerodynamically designed for the best results. Airfoils on the MG Metro 6R4 (left) and Audi Quattro Sport (below) are fully adjustable to optimize the angle of attack for each event

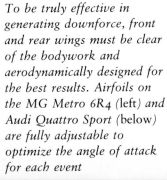

effective in reducing lift because they modify the balance between upper and lower air pressures on the total car. Airfoils operate above the boundary layer of the upper surface in most cases, although they have also been found quite effective in acting as slots to maintain laminar flow close to the body and reduce drag in an otherwise turbulent area.

Deck-mounted rear spoilers are used to induce flow separation. They cause a large air flow 'bubble' just ahead of separation by turning the flow back and 'rolling up' the streamlines into a turbulent ball. This disturbs the relatively smooth air flow pattern that tends to cause negative upper surface pressures and reduces the net lift at the rear. As in the case of front under-bumper spoilers, the effectiveness depends on the height of the device, as does the increase in induced drag it creates.

The strut-mounted detached airfoil has several advantages over the spoiler. Although it also generates an increase in induced drag, its lift coefficient does not change as much with the pitch angle, which makes it a more stable device. It also has the major benefit of being far more easily and quickly adjusted, which allows individual driver handling preferences and different circuit requirements to be accommodated. Team managers often use wind tunnel data during practice to set up cars into optimum race trim by wing angle adjustment (an example of this is described in Chapter 11). High mounted airfoils, however, introduce a pitch moment that tends to lift the front axle and decrease the steering response.

ABOVE RIGHT *This kind of deck-mounted spoiler disturbs the rear air flow to create a large separation bubble ahead of it, reducing the negative upper surface pressures and hence the net rear end lift*

RIGHT *Blocker type air dams can also reduce lift forces by diverting air from under the car and increasing the upper surface pressures. They should really be developed in conjunction with the cooling system for maximum effect*

8 The energy crisis and its effects

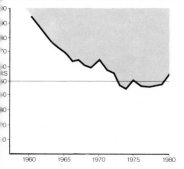

MIDDLE EAST RESERVES/PRODUCTION RATIO

Excessive consumption by the Western World steadily reduced the expected life of Middle East oil reserves. By the time of the first major energy crisis in 1973, less than 50 years supply was predicted by the experts

It is hard to speculate what might have happened to car design if the world had not suddenly, in 1973, been made aware that supplies of cheap, readily accessible crude oil were severely at risk. Car design had for too long been the plaything of the large marketing machine, force-fed by the US multinational giants to create an annual demand for new models that would keep the factory wheels turning and the profits rolling in.

The awakening came with the 1973 Arab–Israeli war, the cutting of Middle East supply lines and the realization that oil resources would not last for ever. Without that first energy crisis, car design could well have swung in another direction altogether, but one which could never have been so long lasting or so forceful in its effects.

Before these Middle East events the availability of crude oil had been characterized by chronic over-supply. Low consumer prices had encouraged the relative wastage that gave many oversized American cars the appropriate label of 'gas guzzlers'. With so little reward for prospecting and drilling operations in difficult geographical areas, like the rich oil fields hundreds of miles offshore in the rough weather of the North Sea, the calculated time left to exhaustion of the readily available supplies fell from 100 years in 1960 to less than 50 years in 1973.

Following the social, political and religious upheavals in the wake of that war, rapid industrialization began to take place in the Middle East oil states, and with it the need for Western capital and equipment. To conserve supplies and provide more guarantees of future security, a steady series of price rises was introduced by the oil producers, raising their share of the revenue from a typical European proportion of 10 per cent in 1965 to over 50 per cent today.

With the rising prices came pressures to reduce fuel consumption and a positive move in design towards more energy efficient vehicles. In the USA a steady programme of dimensional reduction began as the huge cars that had evolved to reflect the successes of the all-American lifestyle shed surplus weight and bulk. Some companies moved faster than others. Some did it better, but none could match the flood of Japanese imports which started to cripple Detroit production. By 1980, one in five new cars in the USA was Japanese, with more than one in three in the western seaboard states. All the large producers were in desperate financial trouble as they frantically re-engineered, redeveloped and retooled.

Fuel economy legislation was introduced as part of a federal energy conservation programme, but it was hardly needed in the face of market pressures. The government objective was to double fuel efficiency in the ten years from 1975 to 1985, based on fleet average consumption during a specified mixed-driving test

Short term action to conserve the fuel used by vehicles was directed towards improved aerodynamic efficiency, as typified by this experimental Ford Fiesta (right) used as a fuel economy research vehicle (FERV). Changes to the front end and the addition of a rear spoiler reduced its drag coefficient by 10 per cent

cycle. And to meet those targets and avoid a supplementary vehicle tax on sales, the focus of attention turned to lightweight structures and low drag body shapes.

European manufacturers staved off similar government rulings by undertaking a voluntary agreement to increase fuel economy between 1978 and 1985 by 10 per cent from a much lower baseline and with much less to work on. Despite the adverse effects of stricter emission controls, they exceeded the target level by 50 per cent, two years ahead of the schedule they had set themselves.

In many ways the changes needed to bring the average drag coefficient of mass produced cars below 0.40 were a painfully long time coming. The full cycle of industry lead times for all-new models is almost four years, with some 36 months being required from final shape approval to Job 1 production. And ahead of that three-year delay a mass of wind tunnel development suddenly became vital. With every manufacturer suddenly beating on the doors of the few full-size facilities in Europe, the achievements possible were undramatic and apparently slow.

Factors affecting fuel economy

For each particular vehicle specification there are four main factors which determine how much fuel it uses. First there is the internal size and power developed by the engine, or its potential to burn fuel, given unrestricted road conditions and determined spirit in the driver. Then, secondly, there is the closely related engine efficiency, or its ability to turn fuel into work, known as the specific fuel consumption (SFC). This depends on the details of the engine design, its internal losses and its combustion characteristics. Different combinations of engine speed and load can correspond to the same SFC, so when each of these points is plotted on a graph of load against speed, a contour map of islands and loops results.

Main Fuel Economy Factors

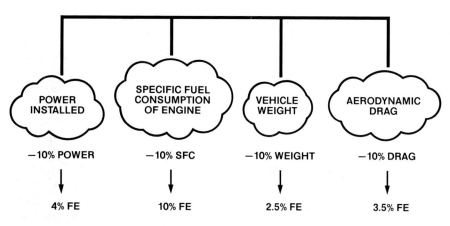

Four main factors determine how much fuel a vehicle uses and how much can be saved by design improvements. Each has a different effect on the total fuel economy (FE), these relationships being for the mixed driving cycle used for certification by the US Environmental Protection Agency

Total drag forces on a car are caused by several different elements of the total design, each of which became the subject of aerodynamic development in response to the need for improved fuel economy. The biggest potential gain comes from the basic body shape, but this is the most expensive feature to change

ISTRIBUTION OF AERODYNAMIC DRAG (Cd)

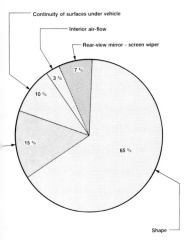

Thirdly, in the lower speed brackets the total vehicle running weight is also important in fuel economy terms, for on that depends most of the rolling friction forces, and mechanical losses are directly proportional to speed. But, fourthly, in the higher speed brackets aerodynamic drag provides more resistance to motion, according to the square of the actual vehicle speed. And although rolling friction is a major factor in a low speed town driving environment, aerodynamic drag becomes dominant from speeds as low as 35 mph in most modern production cars.

In vehicle development there has always traditionally been a trade-off between installed engine power (and the performance levels achieved) and the fuel economy available to a cautious-footed driver. Modern design techniques now approach the problem in the very early paper study stages of development, using computer programmes based on existing test data to predict performance and fuel economy for steady-state operation as well as for any given driving cycle in which speeds, accelerations and gear shift points are defined. Usually these are set by specific technical committees of the European Economic Community (the EEC), or the US Environmental Protection Agency (EPA).

The programme determines the required engine output for the performance level required based on several different inputs. These include instantaneous drag, rolling and acceleration resistance, as well as transmission efficiency data, and the programme uses corresponding specific fuel consumption values taken from SFC maps drawn from bench tests, taking transient effects into account.

To make full use of drag reduction effects, the overall gear ratio of a vehicle must be adjusted to maintain the previous level of performance chosen for each particular car, a science which has become known as Powertrain Matching. If the drag coefficient of a vehicle is reduced without changing the gearing or the engine output to rebalance tractive and resistive forces, the original road load curve (a plot of vehicle resistance to motion on the road) will be shifted away from the most efficient islands in the engine SFC map. Engine efficiency is best at a wide open throttle and reducing the air resistance calls for less engine power (according to a cube law relationship) and hence more throttling (in the case of a petrol engine— diesel engines are different).

So although fuel consumption is reduced by the demand for less power, the deterioration in SFC (fuel consumed per unit of power developed) deteriorates far more. Adjusting the gearing can either put the road load curve back where it was on the SFC map, or allow a better map for a less powerful engine to be substituted. One

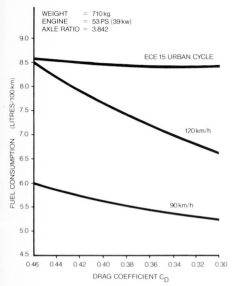

**EFFECT OF AERODYNAMIC DRAG
ON FUEL CONSUMPTION**

WEIGHT   = 710 kg
ENGINE   = 53 PS (39 kw)
AXLE RATIO = 3.842

*The relationship between
drag coefficient and fuel
consumption varies according
to the vehicle speed and
driving mode. This chart
shows the effect on each of
the three official European
fuel consumption figures for
a typical small family car*

way to alter the balance of these factors is to downsize the engine and make it work harder, which can also save weight.

The potential for fuel economy gains by reducing aerodynamic drag as compared to other actions such as weight reduction, engine development or combinations of each reveal some interesting value differences. Reducing engine power alone by 10 per cent, for example, can provide a direct gain in fuel economy of around 4 per cent by allowing smaller valve sizes and less intake throttling under part load conditions (a better set of SFC curves). A 10 per cent weight saving in the US Environmental Protection Agency's combined driving average of mixed traffic cycles results in about 2.5 per cent fuel economy gain. Less weight demands less power to accelerate at the same rate as before, giving cumulative gains when the two are combined.

Aerodynamic drag reductions provide the best of both worlds, giving improved performance and better fuel economy for what can often be absorbed in a new model programme without cost penalty. A 10 per cent drag reduction on the same comparative basis provides around 3.5 per cent fuel economy improvement, while a 15 per cent drag improvement at a steady 75 mph can bring as much as a 10 per cent economy gain.

Drag reductions of this order require totally new vehicle shapes which have not been accepted very readily by the car-buying public. Although smooth, optimized exterior panels can be aesthetically very clean (as on the Porsche 928), taste in fashions for high value products is not easily led into new fields when the typical life-span of a modern car in service now exceeds ten years.

Although there were some good research efforts and some worthwhile gains in the first generation of post-oil-crisis design, it was the second generation models launched in 1982 that made the greatest aerodynamic strides. The 1981 models, like the front-wheel drive Ford Escort, advanced air flow techniques and efficiencies a long way by traditional standards (the Escort's Cd was cut from 0.46 to under 0.40—a reduction of over 15 per cent), and helped steer public taste in the right design direction. But they were totally overshadowed by what was to come.

Two cars stood out from the crowd by the end of 1982, the Audi 100 (5000 series) and the Ford Sierra (Merkur). One became the first production five-seater to reach a Cd of 0.30 and the other showed how 0.34 was perfectly feasible in high-volume, low-cost family cars. Both achieved drag reductions between 24 and 28 per cent that

*These two fuel consumption
graphs (in miles per US
gallon) for similar cars with
different drag values show
how about 4 mpg can be
saved up to 70 mph by as
little as a 15 per cent saving
in drag (from 0.46 to 0.39)*

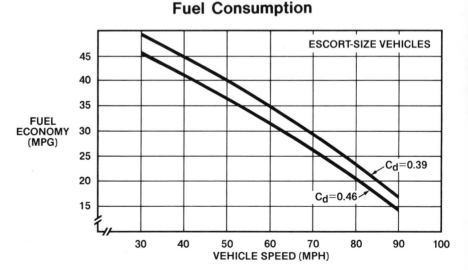

Fuel Consumption

RIGHT *Plotting specific fuel consumption values for each engine speed and load point produces a contour map of loops and islands, over which speed and gear ratio effects can be superimposed. The figures here are for the Ford FERV research vehicle shown earlier*

BELOW *In many ways the 1982 Audi 100 (badged as the 5000 Series for the American market) set new aerodynamic standards which have not been beaten yet. Over 20 body details were optimized in more than 1000 hours of wind tunnel testing to reach a Cd of only 0.30*

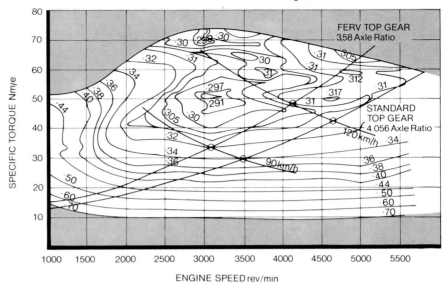

SPECIFIC FUEL FLOW MAP kg/kWh

alone accounted for between 15 and 17 per cent fuel savings at 70 mph. If two million cars in this class on the roads of Britain covering 10,000 miles a year each could reflect these improvements overnight, 100 million gallons of fuel per year would be saved.

Audi engineers tackled the task of drag reduction on the 100 body by starting with an optimized basic shape and manipulating every detail area known to have significant aerodynamic effects. The main differences between the new basic body and that of its predecessor were in the front end treatment, the windscreen inclination, in the planform camber at the rear end and in the A- and C-pillar transitions.

As a first step in the optimization process, the front of the car was rounded out and flowed in with the lamp lenses and bumper moulding to deflect most of the attacking air over the upper surface, each radius and angle being the subject of clay modelling development undertaken during wind tunnel testing. Although in idealized research it was found that a stagnation point as close as possible to the ground gave the lowest drag coefficient, the legal requirements for headlamp and bumper heights precluded the most efficient shape being adopted for production.

A lip seal was added to the front edge of the bonnet lid, closing off the gap to the front grille, and cooling air was ducted directly to the radiator and out under the central portion of the floorpan. The rear edge of the bonnet was swept up to cover the wiper arms and spindles, leaving a full width gap at the base of the 60.5 degrees windscreen, 6 degrees more raked than that of its predecessor.

The function of this gap, apart from partially concealing and totally shrouding the wiper mechanism, deviated completely from established engineering techniques. For many years previously it had been the practice to locate the intake for the heating and ventilation system in a position of relatively high pressure on the surface, usually just ahead of the screen where there was a sudden decrease in air flow velocity (see Chapter 6). This forced ram air through the cabin without the need for the blower to operate once the car was moving, so avoiding one source of tiresome interior noise.

Audi took advantage of the improvements that had taken place in fan blade design to eliminate the drag caused by air entering this way by repositioning the intake in a low-pressure area further back, drawing air into a semi-sealed plenum chamber below. Although the fan was required for the heater to be effective, a useful saving in body drag resulted.

Front and rear screens were bonded flush to their aperture flanges, but the main technical innovation—and one that involved a difficult three-year manufacturing development programme—was the fitment of flush-mounted sliding side windows to all four doors. The solution to the mechanical problem of locating the glass so it sealed against the door frames, but was still free to slide down when required, was to fit mushroom-shaped pegs through the glass with their heads in semi-closed channels.

The stylish, heavily sculptured 'eyebrows' over the wheelarches that had been distinctive visual features of the previous model were smoothed in to form a clean bodyside, pulled out in plan view between front and rear wheels so as to maintain a laminar air flow better. At the rear the Audi featured a smoothly faired plastic underbody moulding for the spare wheel well, which also shrouded the rear silencer and curved gently up to form an extended lower lip for the below-bumper rear apron.

The Ford Sierra design, launched the same year, probably achieved as much in its own way as the Audi even though its absolute drag coefficient was significantly less. While the Audi was developed over five years from more than 1000 hours of wind tunnel testing, the Sierra spent much longer in many more tunnels for reasons of its wider model range and a determination to quote totally indisputable Cd values at launch. In making claims for the new Escort in 1980, Ford had been severely criticized when independent magazine tests on early production cars failed to record the expected results. Sub-standard panel tolerances, vehicle attitude variations and tunnel discrepancies were largely to blame, but a harsh lesson had been learned.

Accordingly all the quoted Sierra drag coefficients were average figures obtained on running prototypes tested in the Daimler-Benz wind tunnel in Stuttgart, and subject to a ±3 per cent tolerance band. This quite acceptable spread actually put the car between 0.33 and 0.35, which really shows the degree of improvement needed to make apparently significant gains.

The Ford Sierra, also launched in 1982, spent even more time in wind tunnels, but was less ambitious in its design objectives. Its Cd was still a remarkable 0.34, more than 20 per cent better than its predecessor

The sporting derivative of the Ford Sierra used a unique double-wing rear spoiler, to lower the drag coefficient and improve stability at high speed. It was dropped from the range in 1985, however, after its styling had been judged by buyers as too extreme

As with the Escort, a great deal of attention was paid to maintaining laminar air flow over the body surface as much as possible and particularly in the area of the rear window and trailing edge of the roof. Here the 'bustle' back (called 'Aeroback' by Ford marketing copywriters), similar to that of the Escort, was found to be most effective at reducing the wake area and hence the drag coefficient. Another important constituent of the overall shape was the marked rounding of the planform (as was the case of the Audi too), both in the lower body and the upper greenhouse area.

Windscreen rake angle was increased from 55.6 to 60 degrees (virtually the same as that of the Audi) and new edge mouldings were specially developed to bring all fixed glass as near the sheet metal surface as possible. New bumper systems, moulded in impact-resistant polycarbonate material, and welded from three plastic sections, were integrated into the lower valance panels front and rear and optimized engine cooling intakes were formed in the basic front end shape.

For the sporting derivative that had become an expected part of each new Ford range, a unique double-wing spoiler like that used on the Probe III design study (see Chapter 9) was added, together with modified front and rear bumper assemblies which deflected the lower airstream more effectively over the wider wheels and low profile tyres of this version. Plastic lower bodyside appliqués pulled the sills out to guide the flow better between front and rear at this level. These changes brought the

Cd down to 0.32 without, it was claimed, any detrimental effects on sidewind stability.

The same was not true of the basic Sierra models, which developed a combination of characteristics in blustery conditions that were frequently criticized by customers and the press. The cause was isolated to an unstable flow pattern around the C-pillar at yaw angles around 15 to 20 degrees. The actual point of detachment 'walked' around the pillar with the wind gusts from somewhere on the rear side window to somewhere on the backlight, creating a twitching kind of weathercock effect.

This problem was overcome in 1984 by the addition of small strakes on the rear edges of the rearmost side window moulding (the sixth light). Although these protruded some 0.7 in. at their maximum section, they prevented the separation point moving about. And as they were beyond the start of the pillar wrapround the cross-sectional area presented to the airstream did not increase. But they did induce a small amount of extra drag, which was offset by the addition of a 1.5 in. deep soft plastic lip to the lower edge of the front bumper spoiler.

The other point where the Sierra achieved more than the Audi was in the availability, from the launch, of a squarebacked estate car version with the same drag coefficient as that of the fastback saloon. Optimized curvature of the near vertical tailgate and glass at the trailing roof edge and rear pillars maintained the Cd

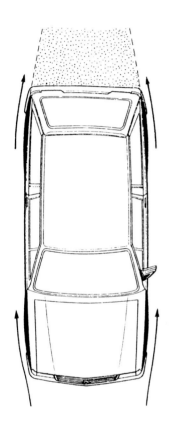

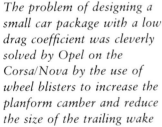

The problem of designing a small car package with a low drag coefficient was cleverly solved by Opel on the Corsa/Nova by the use of wheel blisters to increase the planform camber and reduce the size of the trailing wake

level at 0.34. And to reduce the interference of a roof rack, which is more likely to be fitted to this class of vehicle, a special design using longitudinal stringers and detachable crossbars was offered as an option.

Although its timing was nearly 18 months after the Audi and the Sierra, the Opel Corsa/Nova proved that even small box-shaped cars could also achieve low drag values. Within a total vehicle length of only 142.5 in. (18 per cent shorter than the Sierra and 25 per cent shorter than the Audi 100), a Cd of 0.36 was recorded by using a distinctively new kind of body form that featured blisters over front and rear wheels to allow more than the traditional levels of planform camber.

Ultimate fuel economy machines

Nothing drew the motoring public's attention to energy conservation more than a series of ultimate fuel economy tests held all round the world. Within some quite specific rules, such as a minimum of three wheels, a wheelbase of not less than one metre and a reasonable standard of basic safety requirements, the designers had a

free hand to demonstrate their skills in producing a special breed of vehicle termed 'economobiles'.

With events held in Australia, Germany, Great Britain, the Netherlands, Switzerland and the USA, the competition became quite heated between 1980 and 1984 as the fuel economy figures leapt from under 500 to over 4000 mpg. Many of these economobiles relied on light weight and highly developed engines to record their remarkable frugal records, their designers deliberately ignoring the effects of aerodynamic drag at these exceptionally low speeds.

But Volkswagen and Ford knew better. They took their skeleton structures to the wind tunnel and developed highly efficient teardrop envelopes for them in advanced lightweight plastics and accordingly made it to the record books. The VW effort reached a Cd value of only 0.15, combined with a projected frontal area of only 3.44 sq. ft. It won three economy competitions, raising its ultimate economy from 2495 to 3355 mpg in the process, before being sentenced to retirement in the Wolfsburg museum, its objectives achieved.

Ford's efforts were confined to the annual Shell Mileage Marathon organized by

Volkswagen's 'Economobile', with a Cd of only 0.15, eventually recorded a fuel consumption of 3355 mpg in July 1983, using a 25 cc single-cylinder direct injection diesel engine

The victorious Ford engineering team show the diminutive scale of their 1984 Shell Mileage Marathon winner, UFO2. With a Cd of 0.113, this achieved 3803 mpg powered by a tiny 15 cc petrol engine

Motor magazine in the UK, to find the ultimate that could ever be achieved. Without the constraints of passenger accommodation or even mechanical components and suspension elements to distract the designers, a flood of excitingly different machines appeared each year to cover a distance of ten miles round the Silverstone racing circuit on as little fuel as possible within the set average speed of 15 mph.

The design that stood out from the rest in 1983 and 1984 through its aerodynamic design as much as its proven fuel efficiency (it won the event in 1984) was the Ford UFO2 (Ultimate Fuel Optimizer no. 2) driven by a 15 cc engine. It broke two records, with a fuel economy figure of 3803 mpg and a Cd value of only 0.113. Its shape was virtually a pure teardrop, with the driver lying in a supine position to minimize the projected frontal area, running on three enclosed cycle tyres. As a demonstration of aerodynamic efficiency, it required only 35 watts (0.047 bhp) to propel it at 15 mph.

9 Modern design exercises and concept cars

In the wake of the mid 1970s oil crisis, several manufacturers were spurred on to serious design studies of where the ultimate aerodynamic thresholds of the future lay. The initiative in many cases stemmed from internal company pressures to develop competitive products for the future, when it was widely predicted that oil supplies would become more scarce and more expensive. Some of these projects made a significant contribution to the general understanding of aerodynamic concepts, and a selection of the more radical themes is contained in this chapter.

More or less outside the mainstream of the industry effort was a concept car sponsored by the Federal German Ministry for Research and Technology and involving a study group comprising four automotive engineering institutes at the German universities of Aachen, Berlin, Darmstadt and Stuttgart. Their brief was to design and develop an advanced fuel-efficient vehicle, and to produce four running prototypes. The composite study which resulted was called the UNI-CAR and was aimed at achieving many things, one of the most important being a Cd value of around 0.25 at a time when the average figure for mass-produced cars was somewhere in the 0.43–0.46 bracket.

Work on the body shape was conducted on one-fifth scale clay models and a full-size polystyrene exterior skin in the Mercedes-Benz wind tunnel. Because a compressed time scale was set, and in recognition of the many conflicting requirements in the specification of the project, a mid-size notchback saloon formed the baseline vehicle concept, rather than an advanced aerodynamic shape. While this obviously inhibited the ultimate levels of low drag achieved, it made the task of reaching the final objective a greater engineering challenge.

Shape optimization work was mostly performed on the one-fifth scale clay model, which was designed well enough in the first phase to record a Cd of 0.327 including cooling air flow. In subsequent stages various elements were developed to reduce the drag in steps, followed by a major change to the rear end concept and optimization of that by degrees.

The second primary stage, conducted by many individual wind tunnel tests, reduced the Cd to 0.298. This 10 per cent gain was achieved by several separate actions, including extension of the nose forward to a lower front position, rounding off the front apron and sealing the lower surface of the engine compartment (with outlet ducts in the centre of the under-floor and two outlets behind each front wheelarch), inclining the windscreen to a faster 61-degree rake angle, fitting flush wheel trims and extending the rear notch.

In the third primary phase the tail end was raised instead of being lengthened, with a similar result, and a fastback configuration with rear spoiler investigated.

*Four German institutions
cooperated to build an
experimental study called the
UNI-CAR, first revealed in
public at the 1981 Frankfurt
Show. Its final drag
coefficient as a running
prototype was just over 0.23*

From a value analysis of the design objectives, however, it was then decided to convert the notchback into a square-back estate car based on the same planform, even though the greater wake area produced (and the addition of a second door mirror) increased the total drag by 25 per cent.

Tapering the rear of the roof by 5 degrees and narrowing the rear track slightly so that each of the rear side panels could also taper by 4.5 degrees, according to the well-established principles first expounded by Professor Kamm, brought the Cd back to under 0.30. This configuration then became the subject of a secondary programme to reduce the drag still further and induce higher levels of downforce as an aid to vehicle stability at high speed. Parallel to the development of the clay model, three full-size polystyrene skin surfaces were produced to check the aerodynamic results. These were eventually used for the development of fully functional running prototypes.

GERMAN UNI-CAR DRAG REDUCTIONS

Conditions Scale models (1:5)	Aerodynamic coefficients		
	Cd	Clf	Clr
Notchback saloon (Model A)	0.327	0.045	0.069
Optimized notchback (Model B)	0.298	0.023	0.095
Revised notch profile (Model B)	0.291	0.032	0.033
Fastback saloon (Model B)	0.292	0.032	0.021
Estate car (Model C)	0.364	0.021	−0.217
Kamm back (Model C)	0.299	−0.018	−0.039
(Model C)	0.277	−0.054	−0.050
(Model C)	0.266	−0.052	−0.056
(Model D)	0.243	−0.063	−0.038
(Model D)	0.254	−0.086	−0.061

Full size models (1:1)			
Model A without cooling	0.235	−0.107	0.036
with cooling	0.234	−0.109	0.030
Model C (with suspension and tyres)			
without cooling	0.231	−0.082	0.002
with cooling	0.223	−0.083	0.006
Version D (with prototype underbody)			
without cooling	0.232	−0.093	−0.002
with cooling	0.228	−0.099	−0.009

Volkswagen Auto 2000

Another low-drag concept car to make its debut at the 1981 Frankfurt Motor Show was the VW Auto 2000, claimed to be a project 20 years ahead of the design technology of that time. It was partly financed (5 per cent) by the Federal German Ministry of Research and Technology and was developed with the cooperation of some 30 suppliers to the motor industry.

Auto 2000 was a compact three-door fastback, fitted with either a low-

consumption diesel engine or a petrol engine, and developed as an optimum shape in the wind tunnel before the VW Design Centre turned it into a practical full-size model. Most of the early work was conducted on 1:4 scale models, which in idealized form recorded a Cd value of only 0.16. With wheels, but no doors or windows, and a completely smooth underbody, this rose to 0.18. Then, with more realistic details, like door cut lines, exterior mirrors, a more practical windscreen angle and bumpers able to offer proper bodywork protection, the figure rose again to 0.24.

During the development of this shape into a prototype vehicle a number of totally new aerodynamic concepts was introduced, such as a below-bumper cooling air intake with an outlet in the upper surface of the nose ahead of the engine bay and heater inlets in the tops of the front wings. In its final form, with a carefully optimized belly pan, Auto 2000 recorded a Cd of 0.25.

VERA, VESTA and ECO 2000

While the Germans were developing their UNI-CAR and Auto 2000 projects, the French government agency for energy conservation, which was set up in the wake of the energy crisis, launched an extensive campaign to save fuel and awarded development contracts to Peugeot and Renault to define the 'elements of an economy vehicle' in the form of prototypes, carrying 50 per cent of the financial costs. The Peugeot project was called by the acronym VERA, standing for *Véhicule*

Economie de Recherches Appliquée, and eventually grew into an experimental programme that produced a total of three different concept vehicles. The Renault effort was called VESTA (*Véhicule Economie de Systèmes et Technologie Aérodynamique*).

The first VERA 01 was derived from the Peugeot 305, a family-sized four-door saloon with a Cd of 0.44, and appeared at the Paris Motor Show in September 1980. Its design objectives set nine months earlier were that it should reach a fuel economy saving of 25 per cent. This was achieved by a combination of features including a 27 per cent reduction in drag, a 20 per cent weight saving and a 14 per cent improvement in engine efficiency in conjunction with a 22 per cent increase in the overall gearing (see Chapter 8 for more on powertrain matching).

The changes made to lower the drag coefficient resulted from a total of 14 aerodynamic improvements as listed overleaf, each developed on a special 'aero' prototype before being incorporated into the final functional vehicle. Because the objective demanded techniques that were advanced but capable of being introduced into production by 1985, the modifications were not allowed to change the existing press tooling and consisted mainly of add-on (and in some cases deleted) details. Attention to the rear end air flow around the boot lid and C-pillars, ducted cooling for the radiator and flush wheel covers accounted for most of the improvements made.

VERA 02 was essentially the same car, updated slightly and fitted with a turbocharged diesel instead of an improved petrol unit. It made headlines by

Another study also first shown in 1981 (see previous illustration) was the Volkswagen Auto 2000, used to study the feasibility of many advanced aerodynamic features. Its Cd was 0.25

Peugeot's VERA series of research vehicles were composite prototypes developed as a part government-financed project used to investigate power units, weight-saving potential and aerodynamic improvements. In its second generation form, as VERA 02, the drag of the original 305 was halved

covering a journey from Pau to Paris over French roads at an average of 111 mpg. It was followed in 1983 by VERA PLUS, a more fundamentally modified version in which the windscreen rake was increased to 64 degrees and a full bellypan added, together with a longer optimized nose extension, smoother bodysides with a more cambered rear planform and covered rear wheel cutouts. It achieved a Cd of only 0.22, a 28 per cent reduction on VERA 01 and exactly half the drag coefficient of the original Peugeot 305 that had been the baseline model.

PEUGEOT VERA 01 AERODYNAMIC IMPROVEMENTS

Body feature	Drag coefficient	Step saving
Baseline (Peugeot 305)	0.440	
Raised boot lid + spoiler	0.415	5.7%
Flush windscreen and rear windows	0.408	1.7%
Drip rails + side extractors deleted	0.393	3.7%
Faired in headlamp lenses	0.388	1.3%
Front air dam	0.373	3.8%
Front end gaps sealed + ducted radiator	0.358	4.0%
Bonnet lid lip seal	0.353	1.4%
Faired in rear belly pan	0.343	2.8%
Flush wheel covers	0.333	2.9%
Side window deflectors added	0.318	4.5%
Rear wheelarch fairings added	0.313	1.6%
Vent ducts to front wheelarches added	0.306	2.2%
Rear roof + C-pillar extensions added	0.291	4.9%
Low resistance tyres substituted	0.306	−5.2%
CUMULATIVE DRAG SAVING	0.134	30.4%
VERA 01	0.306	

Renault's efforts were far more radical. Under the same 50 per cent financial backing scheme from the French government, they designed a totally new squarebacked minicar, called VESTA, able to transport four people and luggage with the ambitious objective of beating 94 mpg as the weighted average of the three government fuel consumption figures. In appearance, VESTA was similar to the Volkswagen Polo that appeared a year later, but it lowered the Cd threshold to 0.22 (without cooling airflow) in one huge step.

Like Peugeot's VERA, it used a combination of techniques, employing engine advances with a low-loss driveline and reduced weight to reach the fuel consumption objective. Realistically, Renault engineers at the Paris Motor Show in 1982 claimed only that the driveable front-wheel drive prototype would meet a 0.25 Cd target.

In cooperation with Citroen the French government also became involved in yet another economy car exercise, loosely known as ECO 2000. Over a five-year period from 1976 to 1981 they contributed half of the £30 million programme costs to develop a low-drag design project aimed at the lower end of the market with the same 94 mpg objectives as the Renault. Their first efforts produced a rear-engined minicar with a Cd of only 0.297, but they abandoned this in favour of two other front-drive designs, known respectively as SA 117 and SA 109, both of which were built as prototypes and tested for drag in the St Cyr wind tunnel.

Ford Probe series

While the German and French economy car projects were still being developed in secret, Ford were also working on low-drag shapes in Europe and the USA. Their first public showing in this field appeared at the Frankfurt Show in 1979 as a three-door, four-seater design study named the Probe and roughly based on the dimensions of the Mustang. It recorded a drag coefficient of 0.25 as a non-functional prototype at a time when most of the American production cars had Cd values very close to 0.50. It was followed a year later by a working version, called Probe II, that applied the same advanced aerodynamic principles to a four-door

family-sized saloon, losing some efficiency in the process but nonetheless created a startling effect on the American public, still traditionally inclined towards large, extravagant automobiles.

Probe III made its debut at the 1981 Frankfurt Motor Show, as a Ford of Europe research vehicle. It was based on a fully functional five-seater saloon package intended as a trailer for the visual theme of the yet-to-be-launched Sierra, to condition public taste somewhat towards the shape of low drag cars and to pave the way for the future. Through meticulous wind tunnel development in eight specific design areas, it achieved a truly noteworthy Cd of only 0.22, half the European average for cars in the family car market at that time.

Basic tunnel research work on body shapes for the best aerodynamic results involved a range of vehicle silhouettes and led the design engineers to a semi-fastback style, related to the 'bustle' back of the Escort but enlarged and extended.

It was integrated with a fully covered underbody and developed for a combination of minimum drag and lift coefficients. An additional objective which was fully met was that there should be no dirt deposition above the trailing edge of the tailgate lip below the rear window.

To eliminate all flow disturbing body gaps at the front end, the moulded front bumper was integrated into the upper bodywork and the bellypan, with a matching arrangement for the rear bumper which was fully optimized to induce clean air flow separation in plan as well as in profile. The shape of the front end (partially spherical in section in the lower front area), the small variable-area cooling air intake, the flush lenses for headlamps and turn indicators, plus a windscreen angle of 61 degrees blended to a sloping bonnet with recessed wipers, reduced the Cd from a baseline of 0.44 (the value for the angular Taunus/Cortina) by 23 per cent to 0.34. All window glasses in Probe III were pulled out as close as possible to the surface of

Citroen also developed a series of energy-saving prototypes with government aid in a programme known as ECO 2000. The final version shown here was one of two designs tested in the wind tunnel and on the road to meet the 94 mpg objective

PROBE III DRAG REDUCTION

Body feature	Drag coefficient	Step saving
Ford Taunus/Cortina	0.44	—
Basic shape	0.34	23%
Flush glass	0.33	3%
Shrouded wheelarches	0.32	3%
Streamlined lower sills	0.31	3%
Rear spoiler	0.29	6%
Aerodynamic mirrors	0.28	3%
Venturi belly pan	0.25	11%
Complete underbody cover	0.22	12%
CUMULATIVE DRAG SAVING	0.22	50%

Ford began a series of design studies in the mid-1970s which has so far produced five very advanced concepts under the generic label of Probe. Probe I (above left) was a show car which set the style for Probe II (left), a fully functional five-door developed in the USA

the sheet metal to provide uninterrupted flow round the A-pillars, past the door frames and back down the sides of the body greenhouse. The windscreen and tailgate glass were bonded to surface flanges (a pre-production feature later seen on the Sierra) and the side window mouldings were redesigned to move the glass outwards.

Wheel and tyre turbulence was tackled in an innovative way by reducing the gap between the tyre and the wheelarch. Flexible inserts made from polyurethane were used that could tolerate fouling at full steering lock and full suspension travel without damage. The objective was to maintain laminar flow across the wheel cutout by using a smooth wheelcover and restraining the natural tyre-induced air turbulence. Having robbed the wheelhouse of cooling air for the brakes, small louvres were added to the wheelcovers to catch a controlled amount of air and generate enough surface pressure to induce an inward flow.

Specially designed lower door sills (rocker panels in American parlance) were shaped to reflect the streamlines in this area of the bodyside, collecting the air flow behind each front wheel and aiming it to jump the rear wheel cutout and then follow the rear wing panel partially round the tail. This feature was the ultimate extension of the rear tyre shrouds first seen on the Escort XR3 to offset the additional frontal area of wide, low section high performance tyres. Although it has appeared on many aftermarket body kits, it is not an idea that has been copied by other manufacturers.

The critical area for all semi-fastback body shapes is the tailgate section and the nature of the air flow separation at this point. To reach up further into the boundary layer, reattach the flow to the body and force the air into a more favourable separation pattern, a unique double wing spoiler was developed. Its upper surface deflected air on to the lower one, using carefully developed wing sections and spacing, to reduce the negative pressure on the rear window, so keeping it free from soiling. At the same time this increased the negative lift coefficient at the rear.

To reduce the negative effects of adding two door mirrors, required as a legal necessity in some European markets and to complete the competitive specification in others, their shape was designed with an integral airfoil profile leading gently from the tops of the front wings to the backs of their soft plastic housings. This ensured that there was only a short turbulent wake behind each reflective surface,

which was essentially flat. This resulted in only half the aerodynamic resistance of conventional door mirrors.

The second innovative feature in Probe III was its variable venturi belly pan, which lowered its front end automatically above 25 mph to increase the depth of the front air dam and reduce the duct area for the engine cooling system. Thermal override controls ensured that adequate cooling was available during full load slow driving conditions, as when towing a trailer up a mountain pass, but in normal motorway cruising this device alone reduced the drag forces by 11 per cent.

It was supplemented by a complete underbody cover, developed in the environmental wind tunnel facilities to maintain the required degree of cooling air to the normally exposed underbody components such as engine, brakes, suspension dampers, exhaust system and transmission. The cover was also optimized acoustically to suppress road and aerodynamic noise levels generated in the underbody area. Critically temperature-sensitive parts, like the engine oil pan, differential sump and silencer box were fitted into closely fitting cutouts so that their surfaces were exposed directly to the underbody airstream.

The total drag saving of 50 per cent on the baseline shape was estimated to increase top speed for the same engine output by over 20 per cent, from 112 to 135 mph with 107 bhp output for example. Alternatively, the fuel saved by the reduction in aerodynamic resistance at 80 mph was projected as 27 per cent or about 8 mpg for a car in this class.

Probe IV, which followed a year later, was the Ford US response to the advanced work in Europe. It was, like Probe III, a fully operational running prototype but it used more original mechanical concepts and more futuristic materials to break through the 0.20 Cd barrier and reach a record drag coefficient (measured on a full-size model in the Lockheed-Georgia tunnel) of 0.152.

Although this design study was developed under the control of a Dearborn based engineering team, it was built in steel and Kevlar plastic composite parts by Ford Ghia operations in Turin. Its objective was to demonstrate through advanced engineering, technology and materials that a practical and fully functional passenger car could achieve a drag coefficient previously associated only with land speed record breakers.

After surface development using computer simulations and the milling of clay models directly from the computer tapes, low drag optimization methods were used in the wind tunnel to develop a basic shape that would offer the least possible air resistance under all conditions. Areas subjected to painstaking fine tuning included headlamp lens design, windscreen rake angles, flush side glass, door mirror profiles, underbody components, cut-line location and body gaps, vehicle attitude and fully-covered wheel cutouts.

The result of these efforts was the integration of several additional and unique features, including a low profile powertrain and suspension, automatic optimization of vehicle attitude and front spoiler deployment through computer-controlled air suspension, and the elimination of engine cooling openings by the use of rear-mounted radiator and air conditioning condenser (see Chapter 6). Flexible front wheel covers and a special retractable wiper mechanism were also vital elements in the total concept.

A steeply-raked flush-glazed windscreen at an angle of 67 degrees (6 degrees more than Probe III) and a similarly flush rear window at 70 degrees were supplemented by flush side glass, bonded to the door frames with separate small roll-down access

LEFT *Probe III was a totally European exercise, based on the styling theme of the Sierra which was still under wraps at the time it was shown. It achieved a remarkably low Cd of 0.22 at a time when the European average was 0.44*

BELOW *Probe IV was even more futuristic (and a lot less practical) than Probe III, with enclosed front wheels, a rear cooling system and computer-controlled suspension ride height*

windows set below the natural belt line on each of the four side doors. To present a virtually flat, minimum drag floor to the air flow under the car, the construction of the floorpan was reversed to mount all the reinforcing members on its upper side. Exhaust pipe and coolant transfer pipes to the rear compartment were totally contained within the central tunnel, which also formed a ventilation duct for the engine bay.

To provide minimum installed height and optimized aerodynamic angle of attack with speed, a new design of computer-controlled air suspension was used, with steeply angled front and rear struts, integral damping and variable ride height front and rear. In stationary and manoeuvring conditions, ground clearance at the axle centrelines was 6.5 in. As speed increased and the aerodynamic pressure centre changed, the height of both front and rear suspensions was changed and the variable position front spoiler lowered according to the following calibrations:

PROBE IV RIDE CONTROL CALIBRATIONS

Speed	Front height	Rear height	Spoiler extension
0 mph	6.50 in.	6.5 in.	Stowed
11 mph	5.50 in.	5.5 in.	Stowed
41 mph	3.25 in.	6.0 in.	Stowed
45 mph	3.25 in.	6.0 in.	1 in.
50 mph	3.25 in.	6.0 in.	1 in.
54 mph	3.25 in.	6.0 in.	3 in.

Another critical area of air flow management was created by the wheel cutouts where the distributing effect of rotating wheel and tyre assemblies tends to interfere

with the smooth flow along the bodysides. As a more progressive step than the optimized side panels and flexible lips fitted to Probe III, Probe IV had fully covered wheels front and rear running inside flexible wheel cutout membranes.

Wheel fairings constructed like cycle mudguards with extended skirts were fitted to the front hub assemblies, enveloping each front tyre as closely as possible and moving with the front suspension. The wheel cutout in the body was sealed by a semi-rigid urethane membrane attached to a metal frame for each installation, which enabled removal for servicing or puncture repair.

When the front wheels were turned by the steering, the fairings moved with them to protect the membrane from rubbing contact with the rotating tyre, stretching the membrane material which had a low modulus but enough 'shape memory' to restore the correct body contour after a full-lock turn. And to optimize the air flow around the tyre treads, the ribs and blocks were made uni-directional (i.e. given a directional bias which made them 'handed' to the left or right side of the car).

As Probe IV was a running prototype fitted with an advanced fuel-injection engine, transversely inclined at 70 degrees to the vertical to lower its height by some 6 in., track tests were conducted to find out what fuel economy benefits this dramatic reduction in drag coefficient could achieve. At 50 mph it was shown to require 60 per cent less power to overcome aerodynamic forces than the 1983 model Ford Thunderbird, a new-generation model with a Cd of 0.34. This was translated to a direct fuel efficiency improvement of 45 per cent at a speed of 80 mph.

Probe V was revealed in August 1985 at a news conference in Detroit, where it was hailed as the most advanced concept car in the world, fully functional in detail and with a better drag coefficient than a McDonnell-Douglas F-15 fighter aircraft—0.137. As its significance and detail features are such a strong pointer to future trends, they are dealt with in Chapter 12 where the direction of aerodynamic development in the years ahead is predicted.

The latest Probe V appeared at the end of 1985 with a drag coefficient less than that of a fighter aircraft, and a neat little tail fin for stability at speed

10 Grand Prix and single-seater racing

Aerodynamic development of open-wheeled racing cars has basically followed two separate and almost unrelated routes. In the initial stages of motor sport evolution, the objective was primarily to increase speed by reducing drag forces, while in more recent times the emphasis has shifted to the generation of exceedingly large aerodynamic downforces to improve traction, braking and cornering power. In as much as both causes depend on the science of air flow control, they are similar; in their emphasis, they are totally different.

The first applications of aerodynamic principles were therefore aimed at smoothing out the air flow and reducing projected frontal area. Efforts in this direction began almost 90 years ago and lasted right through until the early sixties. But as knowledge and techniques advanced it became clear that lift was a factor which could not be ignored, especially when idealized teardrop shapes were operated at high speed with the underbody boundary layer in close proximity to the ground (see Chapter 4 for more detail on the magnitude and nature of ground effects).

As early as 1936 Daimler-Benz undertook tests on a streamlined low-drag (the Cd was below 0.20) W125 Grand Prix Mercedes in the Zeppelin wind tunnel. The car was intended to compete in one of the ONS Nazi-sponsored speed record weeks, and it was estimated that the front-end lift could be as much as 447 lb at 224 mph. About 175 lb of lead ballast was therefore added, to maintain stability and steering control at high speed. The same lift phenomenon was later demonstrated, with fatal results unfortunately, when Bernd Rosemeyer's Auto Union attempted to beat a record of 268.712 mph set by Rudi Caracciola in the ballasted Mercedes (further developed by the German Aviation Research Establishment in Berlin to reduce its drag to only 0.157) on the Frankfurt-Darmstadt *autobahn*.

Incidentally, one significant pointer to the future had originated in Gernany several years earlier in the shape of the 1923 Benz Tropfenwagen (teardrop car), in which the driver was located ahead of the engine. By eliminating the propeller shaft and allowing him to sit lower, the frontal area was considerably reduced compared to the conventional single-seat, front-engined racing cars before this (and even many of those which came after).

The mid-engine idea languished until the Hitler period in pre-World War 2 Nazi Germany when Dr Ferdinand Porsche revived it for a new generation of Auto Union racing cars. Post-war the same theme was taken up in Britain by John Cooper for the new class of 500 cc motorcycle-engined single-seater racing cars that brought motor sport back to the tracks when resources and driving talent were at an all time low. These started a trend that was soon carried through first to Formula

Smooth body shapes with an airfoil profile and no aerodynamic aids like this 1950s Vanwall inevitably generate lift at high speed. Lift forces on this car, which needed relatively soft suspension to cope with the often uneven track surfaces at that time, were high enough to increase the ground clearance by at least 3 in.

2, and then Formula 1, as the technical advantages of the mid-engined configuration in both handling and aerodynamics became increasingly clear.

In the late 1950s the mid-engined Cooper 'midget' changed the whole conception of the racing car from a bulky, front-engined monster to a compact, agile machine with a low centre of gravity, small moment of polar inertia, a remarkably compact frontal area and a much more smoothly enveloping, low drag kind of body than had hitherto been the case. When Colin Chapman's new Lotus went a stage further by laying the driver down in a near-recumbent position in front of the low-slung powertrain, the pattern of racing car design changed almost overnight.

Aerodynamics suddenly allowed small cars with low total drag to win races with less power than the traditional machines, so the highly specialized group of racing car designers all went back to their drawing boards in search of new techniques that would put them back in front again. After two generations of 'brute force', science was being applied increasingly to develop new race winners.

Downforce: weight without mass

The idea of using aerodynamic downforces to keep the progressively faster new cars more firmly in contact with the ground, effectively to increase their weight (and tyre friction) without increasing their mass, was almost as old as the Tropfenwagen

At the beginning of the 1960s Grand Prix car designers, such as Cooper, started to put the engine behind the driver, significantly reducing the height of the nose for improved penetration and creating the means for developing the modern wedge profile

and first appeared sporadically during the twenties. Unfairly its progenitors were usually labelled as cranks and ignored, but the idea began to receive credence when Fritz von Opel fitted negative camber wings to his rocket car at the Avus speed events in 1928. It gained respectability when Dr Porsche, no doubt with the death of Rosemeyer fresh in his mind, fitted lateral negative-camber stub wings with 16 degrees negative incidence angles to the Type 80 world-record car he had been commissioned to design for Mercedes-Benz (see Chapter 3).

But the Type 80 was not a Grand Prix car, and road racing drivers accustomed to watching their front wheels at work stubbornly fought shy of any kind of wheel enclosure, claiming it affected their ability to control the car. Even Mercedes-Benz, as recently as 1955, failed to persuade their stars otherwise.

Racing drivers depend on cornering faster than the next man to stay ahead or gain places in the heat of battle, so when a new technological advantage appeared in 1966 it changed the whole direction of development again. This new science generated aerodynamic downforce using a strut-mounted airfoil, shaped and angled to apply negative lift and increased tyre loadings. It was novel, effective and simple enough to start a new generation of racing car design which is still a vital part of Grand Prix racing today.

Aerodynamic wings of this type were first applied in America by Jim Hall and Hap Sharp, with discrete backing from the General Motors research facility who were actively investigating all kinds of race car systems for their competition efforts behind the great 1960s 'horsepower race' to win more sales. They appeared on a Chaparral 2F sports car running in the Bridgehampton CanAm series as a variable incidence airfoil exerting downforce directly on the rear suspension wishbones. The enhanced cornering power and high speed traction the wings provided were responsible for Chaparral victories in many races, including the 1967 Brands Hatch 500-mile event where the effects were keenly observed by most European Formula 1 constructors.

Ferrari engineers were the first Formula 1 team to mount a wing on a single-

RIGHT *After high-mounted rear wings were banned on safety grounds by the racing authorities, there was a spate of aerodynamic 'engine covers', like this rather crude device fitted by Ferrari*

seater car, half-way through the 1968 season. Their approach was retrogressive in a sense, for they supported the airfoil on tubular struts attached directly to the chassis/body structure. This applied the resulting downforce as a sprung weight acting through the suspension springs, which were therefore compressed at high speed. Rates were consequently compromised between the amplitudes available at low speed and the need to prevent crashing through at the much lower high-speed ride height. Chaparral had mounted their airfoil struts to the lower suspension wishbones at a point midway between the chassis pivot and the hub carrier, applying a significant part of the downforce directly through the wheel and reducing the spring rate compromises.

With his typical clarity of vision, Colin Chapman applied a much more scientific wing design to the Formula 1 Lotus soon afterwards. He mounted the airfoil struts directly to the rear wheel carriers to concentrate the total downforce, which amounted to about 400 lb vertical load, through the tyres, thus eliminating the need for spring compromises and actually increasing the effectiveness further. There were other advantages, such as the absence of component forces in other than the vertical direction, and less adverse suspension interaction. The disadvantages were the induced drag of the airfoil and the torsional stresses introduced to the assembly by body roll.

The effect on rear wheel adhesion was dramatic and quickly led to the introduction of nose airfoils, to balance the car more evenly. To prevent them intruding into the driver's forward vision, these were invariably mounted directly to the chassis through the forward body structure. Front and rear airfoils brought lap speeds up in a series of quantum leaps as the idea was universally adopted in various forms, often with a variety of cockpit controls for feathering the attack angles to reduce induced drag on high-speed straights. These first generation wings introduced the concept of negative lift into Formula 1 design and it has stayed firmly as a dynamic aid ever since.

Unfortunately in some cases the constructors took the new techniques to extreme limits without any real knowledge of the forces involved and the mechanical stresses generated in wing components. The engineering standards were marginal on some cars as their designers stretched the devices, in theory and in practice. To raise the airfoil clear of turbulence, many cars mounted them on tall struts which

LEFT *The conception of the modern wing began with this elaborate low speed airfoil fitted to a 1970 Ferrari for the tight Barcelona circuit. Note the trailing edge flaps and slotted leading edge*

*The Chaparral sports racing
coupé was the first car to
exploit downthrust with a
rear wing mounted high
above the body in relatively
undisturbed air. The idea,
but not the standard of
Chaparral's engineering, was
copied by Formula 1
constructors*

took little account of the bending loads generated by the induced drag, their own inertia in corners or the torsion inputs from suspension links. And the sudden unbalanced increase in downforce caused by changing the angle of attack at speed often caused cars to dart about unexpectedly.

As a result of the skimpy construction standards, many wing struts buckled and broke at high speed, causing a variety of incidents and accidents. Some of these were caused by the turbulence created by the slipstreams of other cars, a factor that could hardly be anticipated in the design. While the new wings were working well in still air, their downforce magnitudes were often reduced when overtaking and sometimes even reversed momentarily in the vortex currents that are characteristic of vehicle wakes. And when a car spun backwards the change in the angle of incidence quickly created positive lift.

For all these safety-related reasons wings of this type were banned in the middle of 1969, although subsequently restricted airfoils were allowed provided they met certain well-controlled dimensional limitations. What could not be banned was the lesson learnt. Designers had been shown what aerodynamic downforces could do for them and this part of racing car development could not be thrown away.

At this time several external factors were destined substantially to influence the rate of progress. One of them was the improvement in tyre technology which, in combination with the early types of wing, had effectively doubled the cornering power of cars in the second half of the sixties. This virtually halved the time available for a driver to recover from a cornering situation and led directly to increased pressure on racing safety. Leading designers like Pininfarina 'dabbled' in

LEFT *Matra, with access to aerospace engineers, had variable angle nose airfoils linked to the front suspension before movable devices were banned. As the nose rose above its normal ride height, the angle of attack increased to force it down again*

The typical Formula 1 car of the early 1970s used a modest wing area front and rear, constrained by the regulations on height and width and only allowed as part of the body structure

145

the field with experimental Grand Prix safety cars, and the Grand Prix Drivers' Association began insisting on improved circuit protection in the form of Armco crash barriers, catch fencing and stacked-tyre run-off buffers. At the same time, racing car designers, through the constructors' association, were pressing for smoother track surfaces so they could set the cars up with less ground clearance and reduce the spring problems associated with the use of wings.

The end result of the driver's safety campaign was that long circuits, like the Nürburgring in Germany and the Spa road circuit in Belgium, were eventually abandoned in favour of shorter tracks where the expense of new barriers was less costly. A secondary effect was that track surfaces were improved almost to billiard table standards because their overall running costs were lower and their spectator value from the paying public and for television coverage was higher.

Until the 1970s race organizers had relied on ticket income and a modest advertising revenue derived from trade banners and hoardings displayed on the trackside to pay starting money and make a little profit for themselves. All that changed with the advent of increased colour television coverage commanding large worldwide viewing audiences through live satellite links to many countries. With the multi-million viewers came multi-million revenues from commercial advertising sponsors, followed by a relaxation of the rules covering what could and could not be displayed on the cars themselves. When direct television commercials for cigarettes were banned on health grounds, vast funds found their way into all forms of sport and motor sport particularly.

Inevitably this sudden influx of cash into Formula 1 racing threatened to transform it from a professional sport with a serious role to play in developing road car technology into something approaching the razzmatazz of showbiz. But it also improved the circuits, sharpened competition and gave a massive boost to progress in car design. No longer did the constructors have to work within tight budgets. Instead they had the funds to hire more skilled engineers, to rent major wind tunnels for aerodynamic development and to explore new avenues of design using exotic aerospace materials, all of which had previously been denied them.

And while all this behind-the-scenes action was taking place, technological progress continued in other fields. The flash reaction to the effective ban on wings, apart from a brief flirtation with the largely unknown world of four-wheel drive, was the introduction of wing-shaped engine covers that stayed within the height limit of 80 cm (31.5 in.). But the benefits of free-standing wings in moderation were appreciated and the rules banning their fitment were eventually relaxed within strictly scrutinized conditions. They had to be fixed as part of the sprung structure of the car, without any means of driver control, although incidence angle adjustments during the setting-up of the car by the team mechanics in practice were permitted. Width was limited to 110 cm (43.3 in.) until 1984 and the height of the trailing edge could not exceed the 80 cm quoted above. Within these sensible rules a great deal of valuable development took place, covering such 'free' elements as wing section and configuration, without allowing designers to drift too far towards dangerous extremes.

High wings and the way in which they generated downforces had certainly induced a new approach to racing car design. They had demonstrated that for a modest and containable increase in drag the cornering power of Formula 1 cars could be dramatically improved. They had also made it very clear that given the right kind of conditions—i.e. smooth track surfaces and advanced tyre compounds—there might never be an absolute limit to cornering potential once the

At its ultimate state of development, the full ground effect car used front and rear wings combined with an underbody venturi sealed at each side by sliding plastic side skirts in contact with the ground. This 1982 Tyrrell 012 featured end plates for both front and rear wings, with three separate elements to the airfoil system on the tail

aerodynamic forces had been scientifically harnessed. The higher the cornering speed, the higher the downforces generated and the faster the corner could be taken, perhaps even *ad infinitum*.

All that was needed was the right kind of aerodynamic devices and a superbreed of driver capable of withstanding the enormous levels of lateral g forces generated. As engine power rose it also became clear that, on the almost universally short circuits, with their tight turns and correspondingly short straights, cornering power was becoming more important than low drag. From the start of the 1970s, Formula 1 design became deeply rooted in this philosophy.

Suction ground effects

At this point in time there was a minor, but nonetheless significant, pointer to the future, again devised by the innovative Chaparral design team. At Watkins Glen in 1970 they wheeled out an unusual new car, called the model J2. It featured a ground suction system contained inside a Lexan thermoplastic skirt and powered by an

auxiliary engine. It was, in effect, a hovercraft in reverse, with a pair of fans sucking the body to the ground and driven by a two-cylinder two-stroke 45 bhp Japanese motorcycle engine taken from a Snowmobile.

The concept worked well enough for Jackie Stewart to make the fastest lap in the race, and once again the Formula 1 designers all watched and took note. Brabham copied the principles of the system using an engine-driven fan which they claimed as a 'cooling aid', winning the 1978 Swedish Grand Prix amid protests from other drivers that the device blew out road dirt and grit into their faces and engine intakes. Feelings ran high enough for a permanent ban on artificial ground effects to be introduced soon after.

Aerodynamic progress throughout the 1970s can be divided into three main groups of activity. The first of these, up to 1976, was occupied with the exploitation of wings attached to basically streamlined, low drag bodies. From 1976 to 1980, the bodywork itself began to be treated as an integrated airfoil, controlling and 'managing' the air pressure on the upper surface to assist any wings in their effects, generating a rising wedge shape to the profile view. In 1978 came the revolutionary new Lotus Type 78 and 79 designs, utilizing carefully shaped underbody surfaces to create a venturi that boosted downforces significantly again. These cars, which started another quickly-copied trend, relied on side sponsons shaped like low aspect ratio wings and body sides acting as side plates for sliding plastic skirts. These skirts actually ran in contact with the road surface to form air seals for the underbody duct.

Ground effect cars of this type dominated the Formula 1 scene for the next four years. The perilously high cornering speeds that resulted, coupled with the attendant dangers when a skirt became damaged, resulted in the inevitable ban on skirt systems. It was applied through regulations that specified flat body undersides with a minimum set dimension for ground clearance in the running condition.

In the first half of the 1970s the aerodynamic shape of Formula 1 cars was secondary to the disposition of the main components. The aerodynamicist's task was to clothe the mechanical elements inside a reasonably low drag envelope and then add wings at each end to generate as much downforce as possible. During the era of development much was learnt about wing characteristics for these applications, with all kinds of configuration and airfoil sections being tried, following the hinged Fowler flap or multiple slot Handley-Page principles.

Early in the period, conventional bi-convex airfoil sections were used at high angles of incidence and often copiously slotted. Later, for slower circuits, deeply cambered, low-speed wing sections came into use, usually with a built-in flap. These were installed at a negative attack angle that placed the leading edge higher than the trailing edge, to try and lift it clear of the boundary layer across the body that was usually starting to break away from the surface at this point on the rear of the body. Some of these devices looked like a deep open-topped lateral box, or a section of roof guttering, with little pretence at being aerodynamic in appearance. In function, however, they acted legitimately as wings with flaps extended, in the inverted position. Invariably end plates were used as well, to fence in the extremities of the air flow and add a measure of lateral stability.

At this stage of the art there was a trend to mount the front wings well forward and the rear wings well back, to gain mechanical advantage from the leverage of the forces generated. A secondary advantage of installing the rear wing further back was to try and place it clear of boundary layer turbulence. The limiting factor was the effect of the wing's weight on the polar moment of inertia, desirably low in a mid-engined layout to improve dynamic handling. Most of the possibilities of gain in this way were eliminated in 1974 when the governing authorities for motor sport became concerned about the dangers of rear body extensions and introduced a 1 m (39.4 in.) trailing edge dimensional limit from the rear wheel centreline.

The principle of locating the driver and engine in a streamlined nacelle (referred to as the chassis tub), surrounded by a collection of aerodynamic devices, became the style of the period, making cars look cluttered. The objective was to reduce the frontal area of the two most indispensable components, and leave as clean a wake as possible for the wing to operate within. In this context it began to be appreciated that it was better if the engine configuration could be tailored to the 'tub', rather than the tub to the engine, and a number of constructors even reversed the cylinder heads of vee engines to relocate the cumbersome induction tracts centrally and reduce engine width. So tight was the surface envelope that vee engines came to be preferred because their cross-sections corresponded the most closely with the driver's projected outline.

A subject for debate was the radiator position. Designers had already discovered that aerodynamic benefits diminished along the length of the car and one leading engineer, Tony Rudd of BRM, allocated gain factors according to the position of any feature from the nose. Devices ahead of the front wheels were rated as three compared to a rating of two within the wheelbase and one behind the rear tyres. Thus an air intake, for example, would be one and a half times as effective for the same duct area in the nose as it would mounted further back behind the front wheels. Moving it to the rear, halved its flow rate.

Applying this rule of thumb to the radiator showed that its size and weight could be cut by a third if it could be moved from the best position for vehicle dynamics between the wheels to the best position for aerodynamics in the front of the nose. The solution came from a new design of lightweight radiator with half the conventional weight, developed by Philips in the Netherlands for their Stirling engine project.

There were many variations of nose configuration, one of the most unusual, and also successful, stretching across the full width of the car to give some shrouding of the highly turbulent and drag inducing front tyres. This distinctive style was used in the late 1970s by BRM, March and Tyrrell teams at some time, with the radiators mounted centrally and covered in a top skin which acted as deeply cambered airfoil, generating downforces with good mechanical leverage on the front tyres. Trim tabs on the trailing edge or blanking plates beneath the hollow sections were used to trim the downforce and balance the car. It was claimed that this arrangement improved the air flow over the front wheels and reduced their induced aerodynamic lift, but its shrouding effects along the sides of the bodywork precluded the use of pannier side-mounted radiators. Some designers mounted twin radiators bridged by a low wing section, while Ferrari turned their back on the whole concept with a full width detached airfoil above a wedge-shaped nose.

Tyre lift and drag

At this time Dunlop sponsored an investigation of the little understood air flow around high speed exposed wheels, using the Imperial College quarter-scale wind tunnel with a moving ground plane (see Chapter 4). They found that, apart from around 200 lb of lift being generated by the air wedge forced under the leading edge of the contact patch, known as the 'Flettner' effect, there was considerable pumping

action from the boundary layer carried round by the wheel.

This rotating turbulence moved the separation point of the air flow at the top of the wheel forward, compared to a stationary wheel, considerably enlarging the wake area and increasing total body drag. A secondary effect of the pumping action was that air carried round by the wheel was squeezed out sideways at the rear of the contact patch, creating drag inducing eddies under the car.

Various steps were taken to reduce these effects and even take advantage of them. The Tyrrell team devised a novel system of twin steered front wheels, smaller in diameter than conventional single wheels, mounted in tandem each side. Although the Tyrrell six-wheeler achieved some notable successes, the concept was never copied and was finally abandoned for complexity reasons. The McLaren team preferred to add horizontal baffles ahead of the front wheels, to provide a reaction surface for the air currents as they were swept forward by the front tyres.

With engines breathing some 300 litres of air per second at maximum revs, a lot of attention was also paid to engine intakes during this period. What started out as quite modest air scoops blossomed into great Schnorkels almost overnight. Lotus was the only team to apply aerodynamic science to the shaping of their intakes, combining smooth air ducting with an external airfoil section that added downforce.

The objective of these high intakes was to collect ram air to improve engine breathing, but it was estimated that the degree of supercharging available from the air stream never exceeded 3 per cent at full throttle, and at less than full throttle the extra drag negated any gains. The devices were also prone to collect dust and grit which damaged engines and caused retirements. In 1974 high intakes were banned by new regulations limiting bodywork height to that of the rollover protection hoop.

In 1974, Lotus aerodynamicist Peter Wright laid down a useful set of requirements applicable to racing car design. They were as follows:

1. Downforce should be variable in magnitude and its effective position.
2. A compromise must be struck between high downforce and high drag (downforce induces drag).
3. The car must be provided with a cooling system that can dissipate heat values equivalent to 170 bhp from the engine at ambient temperatures up to 45 degrees Celsius. Cooling must also be provided for cockpit ventilation, fuel pumps, suspension dampers and the brakes, which dissipate up to 85 bhp.
4. The cockpit should be free from wind buffeting, to allow the driver to operate with minimum distraction or fatigue.
5. An airbox must be provided to supply the engine with cool, low pressure air, preferably at stagnation pressure.
6. The car must feel reassuring to drive at high speed, a quality usually derived from high downforce and high drag. Low drag cars tend to feel unstable and the better the subjective feedback to the driver, the closer he will be able to take it to the adhesion limits.

Inverted wing body shapes

To reduce the drag of wide front Grand Prix tyres, the innovative Tyrrell P34 used a twin-steer system shrouded by a full-width nose fairing and box-shaped side sponsons. Although the car won several significant races, technical problems caused the idea to be abandoned

Ground effects on the aerodynamic behaviour of racing cars were first investigated as long ago as 1969, although the characteristics of aircraft wings in close proximity to the ground were studied much earlier (see Chapter 4). At the same time as high wing cars were sweeping the board, BRM decided to try designing a car body that used its own surfaces aerodynamically by adding extensions to the width of the shell between front and rear wheels in plan that were airfoil-shaped in profile. The objective was to generate higher magnitudes of downforce than the limited surface area of separate airfoils allowed. There were no specific thoughts of managing the underbody air flow at this time, although the theory did require higher pressures on the upper surface than the lower.

Under test the proposal worked with a number of distinct advantages: the radiators could be located in the rear of the side extensions (the wing area) with cooling air passing through optimized ducts in the top skin and exhausting in a low pressure area near the rear wheel hubs. A BRM with these features was entered for the 1969 Italian Grand Prix at Monza, but was withdrawn at the last moment. Peter Wright, who conceived the idea, and Tony Rudd revived the concept when they both joined Lotus in 1975, using the quarter-scale tunnel at Imperial College for most of the development work. With a ground clearance of between 1.125 and 1.5 in., a lift/drag ratio of 4:1 was achieved, equivalent to a downforce of 800 lb for a drag penalty of only 200 lb.

These results were supplemented by work carried out in the USA on a racing kart fitted with an aerodynamic undertray and side skirts. Sponsored by Group Lotus of America, the importing company for Lotus production cars at that time, this device demonstrated without any doubt that a combination of a suitably shaped undersurface and skirts—there was no attempt to profile the upper surface—produced a venturi effect capable of doubling the downforce.

Both developments were incorporated in the now-classic Lotus 78 and 79 Grand Prix cars that first appeared in 1978 and immediately dominated the field throughout the season. By the following year other teams had caught up with the technology, copying the principles with many variations on the original Lotus theme.

The general pattern of design established by the Lotus 79 was based on a long box-section, streamlined stress-skin capsule housing the driver, engine and transmission and acting as the main structural member supporting the front and rear suspension systems. Mounted on the sides of this central tub and extending from about 24 in. behind the front suspension to the rear of the engine were the aerodynamic surfaces, like deep stub wings or sponsons, with inverted airfoil sections. In them were housed the coolant radiators in ducts exhausting upwards.

The all-important lower surfaces were carefully formed to act in the same way as the upper surface of an aircraft wing and sealed to the main tub. And the outer ends were closed by flat panels that acted as end plates for what were in effect very low aspect ratio airfoils. To the lower edges of these end plates longitudinal skirts were attached to close off the gap between the wings and the road. Early versions used brushes in rubbing contact with the road surface, but later a durable low-friction plastic called Lexan was used for the contacting lower edge and the whole end plate assembly arranged to slide vertically to accommodate suspension movement.

By closing the gap between the body sides and the road, the width between each skirt and the height between the underbody and the ground was made to act as a high-speed venturi, creating enormously increased downforces that could easily reach twice the mass of the car at speeds around 180 mph. Further downforce was provided by nose and tail wings that could be fine-tuned by adjustment to give the required handling balance. The ratios of nose wing, ground effect and rear wing downforces were approximately 1:4:2. A 1550 lb car, therefore, would generate maximum downforces of about 450 lb from its nose wing, 1800 lb from its underbody venturi and 900 lb from its tail wing.

As the integrated shape of the total car was acting like an inverted wing, one of the problems encountered was the effect of transient suspension changes affecting the pitch attitude, which altered the angle of attack and moved the centre of aerodynamic pressure either forwards or backwards along the car. In some situations a resonance developed to create an unsettling 'porpoising', or rocking-horse motion that disturbed the aerodynamics and the driver. One solution was to set the car suspension with very little wheel movement, but in most cases trimming the balance of front and rear airfoil angles acted as an effective pitch controller and damped the characteristic to within reasonable and acceptable limits.

Most racing car aerodynamicists' calculations are based on the plan area of the car body, which forms the wing area of the total airfoil and therefore conditions the amount of lift to be expected, and the projected frontal area of the total car including wheels and tyres, which determines the drag forces. Within the confines of the mechanical layout and the rules of construction, there is not a great deal of scope for developing low coefficients of drag.

To control the degree to which aerodynamics could be exploited, the Formula 1 World Championship Regulations as laid down by the governing body FISA during the period in question restricted the plan area to 70 sq. ft and the frontal area to 18

By 1981 Grand Prix cars were using the body sides for aerodynamic effect in addition to front and rear wings. This French Ligier featured a huge front wing, side skirts and a rear airfoil to generate maximum downforce

sq. ft. The plan area does not include the wheels, but the frontal area does and is measured down to ground level to include the underbody area. Additional regulations, as already mentioned, restricted the height and width of the rear wing and the position of its trailing edge relative to the rear wheel centreline. There were also controls on the width of the bodywork nose.

Such is the speed of development under the pressure of motor sport competition that the domination of events by the Lotus 79 was shortlived. It was replaced quite quickly by the Type 80 with longer, cleaner underbody surfaces and with the side sponsons extended past the rear suspension to give an airfoil surface almost two thirds the length of the car. Although it was a logical improvement with a refined entry for the underbody venturi using sideskirts under the wedge profile nose, it was never very successful in races.

Cornering speeds of the skirted cars with ultra-wide, high friction tyres became dangerously high to the point where a damaged skirt could, and sometimes did, result in disastrously serious consequences if the driver was not aware that his cornering ability had suddenly diminished. Inevitably, despite protestations that it was better to restrict the plan area further than simply to ban the concept, skirts were completely outlawed in 1982 and a tyre width limit also introduced. But the progress made in the general science of racing car aerodynamics did not die and there were impressive goals for the new generation of unskirted cars to aim for.

ABOVE LEFT *This Tyrrell 009 shows how the side skirts run in contact with the ground to seal the underbody venturi and generate negative air pressure. Front and rear wings at this time were relatively small*

The latest approach for the 1985 season by Tyrrell (left and Renault (above), after side skirts had been banned for a year, generated most of its downforce from its front and rear wings, assisted somewhat by the wide sponsons and flat underbody. Scientific development in moving-floor wind tunnels provided about as much total downforce as the earlier skirted designs

The effectiveness of skirt technology is well illustrated by looking at how lap speeds increased round three typical slow, medium and fast circuits. Between 1976 and 1982 lap speeds at the tight American Long Beach race track went up by 20 per cent, those at the medium speed Austrian Zolder circuit increased by 14 per cent and those at the relatively high speed Silverstone circuit rose 15 per cent.

The elimination of skirts through regulatory controls spawned one very original and effective aerodynamic concept, again from Lotus who, in 1983, built it into their Type 88. It sought to maintain the objective of sliding side skirts—to keep the lower edges of the bodysides in contact with the road and allow a measure of suspension movement—through a twin chassis design. It was a typically ingenious solution that suspended the aerodynamic surfaces of the body directly from stiff springs attached to the wheel carriers, with the driver's cockpit, engine and transmission mounted in a normally sprung skeleton inside the outer shell.

In the eyes of the Lotus designers it effectively evaded the letter of the regulations that prohibited side skirts and proved itself able to generate high downforces and give the driver a reasonably comfortable ride. In the view of the authorities, with whom Lotus fought a long, hard political battle over the legality of the Type 88, it did not qualify as an unskirted design.

Today's Grand Prix cars are therefore devoid of skirts and end plates for their wing-shaped body profiles, which are limited on width and on the maximum size of tyres permitted. The current rules stipulate that the underside of the hull shall be flat for the full length between the wheels, and the width of the rear wing is also limited. Designers evacuate the underbody area now by extending the undertray and the undersurfaces of the side sponsons into the area behind the rear wheels and

turn trailing edges up to act as diffusers.

At medium racing speeds of around 100 mph current Formula 1 aids generally induce equal amounts of downforce and aerodynamic drag, with typical levels being of the order of 300 lb. At the very high speeds possible on some circuits—as much as 200 mph can be reached with today's engine powers—the lift/drag ratio of these devices can reach 2:1 with downforces as high as 1200 lb.

Because of tyre drag from the exposed wheel layout of a Grand Prix car more than anything else, drag coefficients are actually very high by the standards of sports racing cars with enclosed wheels, or production road cars, being in the region of 0.8 to 0.9. Extraordinarily high engine power from the turbocharged engines combined with the inevitable progress of development in suspension and tyre design is allowing lap speeds now that are higher than those ever achieved by skirted cars up to the time they were finally banned in 1982. The big question for the future is how much further they can be allowed to rise before additional restrictive measures are introduced to restore safety levels once again.

In other single-seater classes, like the Formula 3 Championship Ralt RT30 (above) and Formula Turbo Ford (right), the technology used to develop aerodynamic downthrust was a follow-on of Grand Prix practices

11 Sports and saloon car racing

In the field of sports and saloon car racing, regulations on the construction of the machines involved determine precisely what may and what may not be undertaken to reduce aerodynamic drag and to generate downforces for increased traction in corners. In the classes of sports car racing where at least some attempt is made to create a relationship with actual production cars there are strict controls. In the design of cars for 'prototype' categories the rules are much more open to innovative and extreme interpretation. The possibilities in production saloon car racing, by definition of the vehicle class, are considerably limited.

At the end of 1967, when most long distance races had previously been contested by specially created machines of unlimited engine capacity, the International Sporting Commission of motor sport's governing body, the FIA, decided from the start of the following season to change the rules. There were to be two new classes for world championship sports car racing: a relatively free category for 'Prototypes' under 3 litres engine size weighing at least 650 kg (1433 lb), and a more restricted category for 'Homologated Sports Cars', up to 5 litres weighing at least 800 kg (1764 lb), of which at least 25 examples had to be manufactured and scrutinized for compliance.

For the World Rally Championship (WRC) and the European Touring Car Championship (ETC), two more categories were introduced for 1982: Group A for saloon cars of which more than 5000 had to have been made, and Group B for saloon cars of which at least 200 had to have been made.

So the past 20 years really represents the period in which the science of aerodynamics has become crucial to the success of the design teams involved in world class racing. With the new 1967 engine size limits came an effective ceiling on engine power, within the technology available for racing engines running in naturally aspirated form (unlike the turbocharged engines under 1.5 litres capacity which later dominated Formula 1). And with engine power restricted the only route to higher lap speeds was through reduced bodywork drag and faster cornering speeds. When turbocharging proved itself so effectively in Formula 1, the technology cascaded down to the sports car field and changed the direction of development yet again.

But the period through the 1970s in Europe was the creative era for ultimate car aerodynamics in the high speed regime, where peaks in excess of 240 mph were reached regularly on road circuits like Le Mans. It seems hard to credit now that horsepowers have been capped, but the twin turbocharged 5.4-litre Porsche 917 specifically developed for the North American series of CanAm races against cars up to 8 litres capacity actually developed 1100 bhp. These cars, which in

ABOVE RIGHT *Even in the heyday of post-World War 2 sports car racing, aero-dynamics began to shape the bodywork of out-and-out competition machines, like this smoothly enveloping Jaguar C-type developed from the classic, but far more contoured XK120. C-types and the later, more aerodynamic D-type, were extremely successful at Le Mans*

BELOW RIGHT *Thirty years later the shape of endurance racing cars had changed almost out of recognition, with minimum ground clearance and narrow cockpit bubble canopies. This 1981 Ford C100 was powered by a Cosworth DFL 3.9-litre V8, but never developed to its full potential*

In 1980 a French Rondeau-Cosworth won Le Mans and in 1982 the World Endurance Racing Championship. It typifies the state of racing car aerodynamics at the beginning of this decade, with a low drag envelope developed for maximum downforce with the aid of a horizontal front spoiler and a rear wing (and stubby rear fins for stability at high speed)

By 1985 endurance racing car
shapes had not changed very
much compared to 1980
designs, as this Group 44 Le
Mans Jaguar prototype
shows. The nose has a
cleaner profile (with air
outlets through louvres in the
front wings) and the rear
wing is more detached

Aerodynamics in power boat racing has become increasingly important, with wings being used to generate lift to pull the boat clear of the surface friction. Unlike the high speed racing car, tail fins are not needed on boats because of the stabilizing effect of the underwater propeller

automotive terms can only be regarded as freaks despite their remarkable achievements, did serve as useful tools in the overall development story. They will be discussed later in this chapter.

The fundamental parameters within which racing car development takes place have not changed much since the seventies. Within any set power limit, satisfactory top speed can be obtained only by careful aerodynamic development of the bodywork shape to achieve both low drag and acceptable driving qualities at high speed. And the key difference between Formula 1 and sports car design hinges around the inherent stability of any shape in relation to its drag.

It is a characteristic of all bodies propelled through a fluid (either a gas like air or a liquid like water) that the lower their resistance to movement, the more sensitive they are to lateral forces. In the case of water, the conditions are easier to visualize. The more a powerboat's hull comes out of the water to reduce its drag, the less control there will be over its direction of travel. When the ultimate is reached, as in the case of a hovercraft where surface friction is almost zero, directional stability is only obtained by aerodynamic control surfaces mounted on the superstructure.

In Formula 1, where drag coefficients as high as 0.85 or 0.90 can be tolerated, stability will be a natural feature at high speed, supplemented where necessary by development of the body into the form of an inverted wing section (see Chapter 10). In sports car design, the influences of lift and sideforce are much more critical because the Cd is usually less than half that of an equivalent open-wheeled Formula 1 machine.

Compared with an aircraft, which has its aerodynamics dedicated to the primary task of providing lift with acceptable pilot control through a range of flying attitudes, the racing car is extremely complex. It is inevitably a cluttered shape, constrained by the layout of its mechanical components, the provision of cooling air flows for engine and brakes and the need for the wheels to be in contact with the ground. Yet to be competitive in races it must reach speeds in excess of those achieved by many light aircraft.

Air resistance is proportional to the square of the speed (see Chapter 2), and engine power to the cube of the speed, which means that it takes eight times the power to double any speed achieved. Increasing the top speed of a typical sports car from 165 to 188 mph with the same engine power therefore requires a drag reduction of 33 per cent, from 0.40 to 0.27 for example. Such an improvement was achieved by Porsche in the transition of their Le Mans Performance Index winning cars in 1967, from the short-tailed Carrera 6 to the long-tailed 907, which also had its frontal area reduced, largely by substituting 13 in. diameter wheels for the original 15 in. size.

Development techniques

The process for this kind of development starts (like so much of car design) from the hardpoints of wheelbase, track width, tyre size, engine package, cockpit space and the bodywork limits as laid down in the appropriate regulations. From these parameters a model of the shell and underbody is built, usually to a one-fifth scale, for initial wind tunnel testing. First an approximate form is shaped in clay and wood, both materials being easily worked and well suited to the representation of the detail fittings and panel contours.

For simplicity in the early stages, design requirements such as suspension movement, the lower side of the engine and air ducts are not included but left for future development on the full size model. As in the development of optimized shapes for production cars (see Chapter 5), there are scientific rules to follow in achieving low drag. Flow must be smooth and vortex-free over the body as far as possible, and natural laws must be used to advantage where possible. Air, for example, can withstand high acceleration of its velocity without turbulence, but only low decelerations. So although there can be relatively sharp entry edges in the forward area, trailing edges must be carefully controlled and all tapering panels at the rear developed to minimize the cross-section of the inevitable wake vortices.

As the magnitude of the Cd depends very strongly on the size of the tail cross-section at the point of flow separation, the search for low drag led to a fashion in the late 1960s for long-tailed high-speed cars. Some of the more adventurous designers, like those at Porsche, developed alternative tail sections for the same cars, depending on the circuit involved and the speeds attainable. The compromise had always to be made between the surface friction created by a long tail and the drag reduction achieved, taking full account of the reduced stability of a long tail from its rear weight bias and the effects of the lower drag already mentioned.

For a while, Porsche actually prepared interchangeable nose and tail sections during their wind tunnel development of the racing 907 coupé, selecting the most

In the early days of GT racing the objective of a rear lip spoiler was to increase rear end pressures by lifting the streamlines and increasing the air pressure. Ferrari GTOs and Ford GT40s were designed on these principles

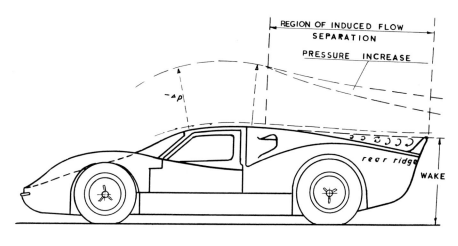

favourable for future work and even trying the alternatives at Le Mans during practice sessions. The complexity of such schemes and the difficulties of optimizing the car's gearing to the theoretical differences in drag, plus the increased hazards of stability reductions, particularly in the intermittent gusts created when passing slower vehicles, led to simpler solutions being found.

Different nose shapes influence the overall flow envelope so strongly that they can change lift conditions at the rear axle significantly. Nose and tail sections must always be developed together as part of the central body section, as the wheels and wheel housings exert considerable influences on the flow between front and rear of the car. Flow must be led off the nose gently to allow the tail section to function effectively. If flow separates too early, laminar flow will not be maintained over the tail.

Actual tunnel testing usually involves a series of techniques, designed to provide empirical data on air flow from visualization through smoke streams applied across the boundary layer and by surface markers such as artists' pigments suspended in water and glycerine. Additional information can also be obtained from pressure tappings across the model surface, a typical one-eighth scale model, for example, being fitted with up to 100 tappings from which maybe 1000 or more pressure coefficients would be recorded.

The results of tests carried out in 1969 by Kingston-upon-Thames Polytechnic for Piper Cars on a model from which a Le Mans entry was later developed, showed that, as the angle of incidence was increased, the negative pressure coefficients on the upper surface increased rapidly. The stagnation point therefore moved forward, passing over the nose and on to the lower surface, converting downforce to positive lift. Too much rear axle downforce can lift the nose and induce this kind of a transition at speed.

This one-fifth scale model of the Jaguar Group C racing car was developed with Tom Walkinshaw in the Imperial College moving floor wind tunnel. It is typical of the detail necessary to produce representative results. Note the integrated front wing and detached rear airfoil with vertical end plates for high speed stability

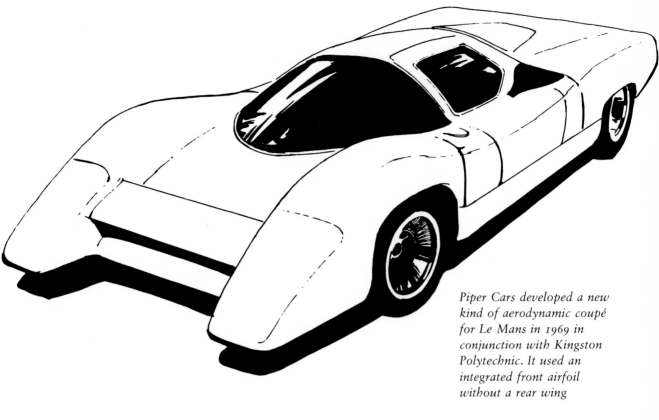

Piper Cars developed a new kind of aerodynamic coupé for Le Mans in 1969 in conjunction with Kingston Polytechnic. It used an integrated front airfoil without a rear wing

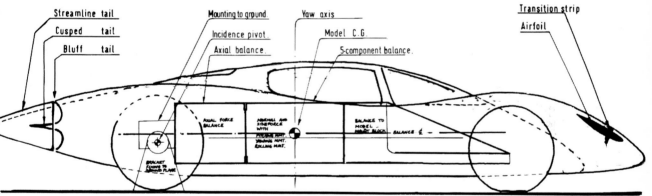

As well as the adjustable airfoil mounted in the nose intake, the Piper GT was tested with three different tail profiles – vertical bluff surface, sculptured 'cusped' contour and pointed 'streamline' extension

Bodywork changes developed by Porsche for the 907 achieved a reduction in total body drag of 7.5 per cent, but increased the lift on the front axle and cut the lift on the rear axle. An alternative nose/tail set was even better on drag (10 per cent lower than the control model), maintained the original slightly negative front axle lift coefficient, but turned the rear axle lift sufficiently positive for an add-on rear spoiler to be necessary, which brought both lift coefficients close to zero.

From the 907, the 908, 909 and 910 were developed in the highly specialized field of ultimate performance machines, the latter types being designed more for the short, sharp thrust of the European Hill Climb Championship than the high speed thrash of endurance racing. It was the 917 that not only totally dominated sports car events of the early 1970s but took the aerodynamic art to new levels of achievement.

165

Porsche 917: a case study in racing aerodynamics

The basic version of the Porsche 917, as homologated in the 25-off sports car category for racing in 1969, had a coupé body with a large plexiglass rear window to the cabin that sloped gently towards the tail, which finished in a short cut-off vertical face. To this a long tail extension could be bolted for high-speed circuits with a vertical fin each side connected by a horizontal airfoil. At each end of this surface was an aircraft-type trim tab connected to the rear suspension so that the downforce generated was proportional to the suspension movement. It increased when the rear end lifted under braking and decreased when the rear end squatted under acceleration. The effect was to stabilize the car aerodynamically in pitch during straight line running and to oppose roll forces aerodynamically in corners.

Very soon after the 917 was homologated in this form, the CSI banned all forms of movable aerodynamic devices, although 917s with these stabilizers were allowed to run at Le Mans that year under a special dispensation. But the long tail introduced considerable instability, for the reasons already outlined, which was only cured eventually by extensive track testing followed by wind tunnel development of a new rear end shape.

The solution was a new departure for aerodynamic design with a rear engine cover that was formed by an upper surface and very little else. From the cockpit sides the bodywork swept back and up to form an integrated rear spoiler, below which the air was free to circulate freely. This raised the Cd from 0.40 for the original short-tailed coupé to 0.447, with a front lift coefficient of −0.031 and a rear lift coefficient of −0.287. An alternative short-tailed 917, with a separate rear airfoil developed by John Wyer for his Gulf-sponsored entries, returned a Cd of 0.438 with

10 per cent more rear downforce (−0.313), but 42 per cent less front downforce (−0.018) due to the fulcrum effect of the change in balance.

For the 1971 season Porsche undertook more development work in the Stuttgart wind tunnel, which resulted in stubby tail fins being added (to improve straight line stability) with small adjustable-angle spoilers at each end of the upswept tail surface. This cut the Cd to only 0.386 while maintaining lift coefficients of −0.037 front and −0.228 rear. And when large engines were banned in Europe, the focus of development shifted to the USA where a full 1972 racing season was planned for a model known as the 917/10.

Racing car type	Cd	Clf	Clr
917K	0.447	−0.031	−0.287
Gulf 917K	0.438	−0.018	−0.313
CanAm 917/10—open cockpit	0.590	−0.071	−0.800
(with concave nose)	0.565	−0.128	−0.690
(final form)	0.588	−0.248	−0.746

The problem with all the European cars was their acute sensitivity to changes in the angle of incidence, caused by the normal pitch motion of the suspension. The slight downforce at the front (with a value of only about 40 lb aerodynamically and well under half the car's weight statically), for example, was frequently being converted to lift, with very disturbing effects on stability and handling. To improve this

LEFT *The second version of the Porsche 917 used the engine cover as an integrated rear airfoil after the original movable rear wing was banned by the introduction of new regulations*

BELOW *Considerable wind tunnel development was carried out on the Porsche 917/10 to optimize the balance of front and rear downforces by fine tuning the various angles of front and rear airfoils. In this original CanAm version the air was ducted through louvres in the tops of the front wheelarches*

characteristic, the front and rear horizontal surfaces were reshaped to be slightly concave, which increased the Cd of the long-tailed car by 10 per cent.

For the CanAm series a new body was developed, lighter in weight through the use of composite materials and with an open cockpit, to be more competitive on critical acceleration in races where horsepower, more than outright top speed, was often a more important factor. With wider wheels to provide the traction needed to handle outputs already approaching 1000 bhp and the inevitable turbulence of the open roof, the Cd rose by over 30 per cent.

It was this modified 917L which was used as a kind of racing test-bed in preparation for the 1972 CanAm racing season in North America. The lift coefficients for the first version of the 917/10 quoted in the table (on the previous page) actually translated to a front downforce at 200 mph of 87 lb and a rear downforce of 980 lb, which required incredibly stiff spring rates to withstand the vertical loading and incurred a considerable ride penalty in a car weighing only 1638 lb without fuel.

Although the imbalance in downforces (that at the rear was more than 11 times that at the front) produced a stabilizing degree of understeer in the high-speed turns common to American race circuits, it was generally felt to be undesirable. So a new approach to front downforce was developed using a bank of four airfoils acting as slats each side of the nose ahead of the wheelarch, contained at their ends by 'fences' to prevent air spillage and adjustable during testing sessions. The lower three could be set together as an assembly, and the upper one was adjustable individually. They were supplemented by a rear airfoil with a trailing edge flap, adjustable in two parts. In this trim the 917 logged a Cd of 0.565, with a more balanced front/rear downforce ratio of only just over 1:5.

Considerable development was carried out on this arrangement, in an all-out quest to optimize the downforces with a minimum drag penalty. The results shown in the table reveal how the Cd value for the total car crept up during development of these devices by almost 15 per cent on the base level, which itself was over 50 per cent worse than the ultimate achieved on the long-tailed Le Mans cars, before a new approach to the problem brought it back within bounds.

The last step in the table is really the most interesting of all. Instead of continuing to play around with the front slats and the rear airfoil, the engineers took another look at the pressure distribution over the nose of the car and took many readings of the pressure coefficients within the airfoil recesses on the front wings. They found that although the desired high pressure existed in the forward part of the slat assembly, there was considerable negative pressure towards the rear where the air was creating a venturi effect as it flowed out and over the upper wheelhousing.

These results led to the removal of the slats and the substitution of simple louvres in the low pressure area to allow high pressure air from inside the wheelhouse to fill the depression. The final effect was an equivalent level of front downforce combined with a 9 per cent reduction in Cd.

Some interesting facts emerged from the Porsche experience. The first was that within any Cd bracket the total of front and rear downforces do not vary very much—from −0.818 to −0.994 in the Porsche example, although the front/rear balance changed from 1:5.4 to 1:3 on the ultimate version. The second conclusion is that the penalties of generating downforces more than the weight of the car are extremely difficult to contain within reasonable Cd limits. And the third fact is the simple truth that in aerodynamics there are several different ways of achieving the same result.

By 1985 the 917 had been replaced, first by the 936, and then by the 956 shown here winning at Le Mans. The design links with the historic 917 clearly show despite the concave front profile and detached rear wing

SPORTS AND SALOON CAR RACING

So, for the following year's CanAm season, Porsche went back to the drawing board and submitted the aerodynamic development to the French-based design house SERA, who embarked on a new development programme using the Eiffel wind tunnel in Paris. The 917/30 was the result.

AERODYNAMIC DEVELOPMENT OF PORSCHE 917/10

Trim conditions	Cd	Clf	Clr

Front—triple slats, 25°30'
    —aux. flap, 28°30'
Rear—main airfoil, 15°30'
    —aux. flap, 31°30'
	0.565	−0.128	−0.690

Front—triple slats, 30°00' aux. flap, 41°40'	0.580	−0.192	−0.674
Front airfoils—forward 125 mm —down 40 mm	0.580	−0.180	−0.662
Rear airfoil—replaced by 3 slats	0.608	−0.210	−0.677
Front airfoils—up 150 mm	0.626	−0.317	−0.600
Rear—main airfoil, 20°00' —aux. flap, 30°00'	0.648	−0.196	−0.740
Front—no airfoils, louvres at rear of wheelhousings	0.588	−0.248	−0.746

The front panels remained unaltered from the 917/10 design, apart from a smoothing of the horizontal front spoiler and raising of the wheelarches to allow air to circulate with the tyres more freely (and flow more easily out of the high pressure louvres in their upper surface). But the rear half of the body was radically changed, with integrated side fences that swept up at the rear to form short vertical fins between which the rear airfoil was carried.

The results were frankly disappointing, although the car's sensitivity to incidence angle changes was much less marked. So a programme of track testing began to make further improvements. It resulted in the grafting of the old 917/10 rear airfoil to the new SERA body, which was also lengthened in the wheelbase by some 7.5 in. to reduce weight transfer effects. To cope with the high downforces generated (by now comfortably in excess of the car's starting weight with full fuel tanks), advantage was taken of the higher wheelarch clearances of the new shape to increase the total suspension travel available to a very generous 6.3 in.

In this form the 917/30, with its 5.4-litre turbocharged engine developing 1100 bhp, was probably the most powerful racing car ever to compete in circuit races. It recorded a lap time at the banked Talledaga track equivalent to 221.120 mph and allowed Mark Donohue to win the 1973 CanAm Championship with ease.

AERODYNAMIC DEVELOPMENT OF PORSCHE 917/30

Trim conditions	Cd	Clf	Clr
Rear—main airfoil, 22°	0.501	−0.339	−0.418
Rear—main airfoil, 23°	0.509	−0.343	−0.456
Rear—deeper airfoil, 25°	0.642	−0.258	−0.830
After track development—long tail, 60 mm front spoiler, NACA airfoil from 917/10			
Rear—main airfoil, 7° —aux. flap, 26°	0.520	−0.322	−0.548
Rear—main airfoil, 8° —aux. flap, 33°	0.576	−0.265	−0.758
Rear—extended deck with 80 mm spoiler	0.575	−0.284	−0.760

Saloon car racing: less scope, more detail

Changes permitted to improve the aerodynamics of touring and saloon cars within the official definitions of the classes involved are very small indeed. The attention of designers and race tuners is therefore directed towards many different details that hopefully add up to a useful net gain. Because the nature of the developments borders on the 'legal' limits of the rules, only general details are given of the cars used in the two examples quoted to illustrate techniques.

Cars intended for production model categories of racing are inevitably offered, at

RIGHT *In Group A saloon car racing there is very little opportunity for aerodynamic development of the body. This Ford Escort RS Turbo set a new lap record for its class at Silverstone first time out in 1985, using essentially standard bodywork features*

BELOW *Small but significant bodywork changes were allowed to the Andy Rouse Sierra Turbo which won the British Saloon Car Championship in 1985. Based on an XR4i, the body features a modified nose moulding with low radiator intake and special ducts to supply brake cooling air each side*

least in one model derivative, with some kinds of aerodynamic aids that are unlikely to have been optimized in the wind tunnel. For sound marketing reasons, many body features are designed more for their showroom appeal than for their aerodynamic performance. And for equally sound manufacturing reasons, or functional considerations in the customer's hands, the effect of these aids is often less than the ultimate that can be achieved by detail development.

The starting point for touring and saloon cars, it should be appreciated, is a body shape with a reasonably low drag coefficient (usually somewhere in the 0.35–0.42 bracket), but with quite considerable levels of natural lift front and rear. A typical saloon or coupé, for example, is likely to have around 150 lb of positive lift on the front axle at 100 mph and as much as 100 lb on the rear axle at the same speed. The first exception to this rule is the Ford Sierra RS Cosworth, which actually generates a net downforce in standard form from its deep front air dam and high-mounted rear spoiler.

To illustrate the differences obtainable through detail development, the moulded rear spoiler fitted to the tailgate of the high performance derivative of a Rover 3500 is used as an example. It is a car which was proved to have considerable race-winning potential for a few brief seasons and on which a great deal of development time was spent in wind tunnels to improve its aerodynamics.

In standard form this particular saloon, fitted with its optional rear spoiler, has a Cd of 0.408, a front lift coefficient of 0.311 and a rear lift coefficient of 0.039. After development in a wind tunnel, seven quite small detail changes reduced the Cd by 4 per cent to 0.391, the front lift coefficient by 33 per cent to 0.208 and the rear lift coefficient by 25 per cent to 0.029. Similar work on a Capri 3-litre coupé reduced the Cd by 6 per cent, the front lift coefficient by 50 per cent and converted the rear lift coefficient from a small positive value to an equal negative value.

The steps taken in each case are listed in the tables of results. They both show how a succession of small actions can be added together to provide a significant result. In the case of the saloon, it increased peak speed on the fastest straight by about 8 mph, partly through the drag reduction and partly through the higher corner exit speeds it allowed.

ABOVE *The same restrictive regulations as in Group A saloon car racing apply to international rallies in the Group A class, where at least 5000 examples must have been produced for the car to be homologated. Rover 3500s like this works car are more suited to track events than special stages on rough roads*

AERODYNAMIC DEVELOPMENT OF RACING SALOON

Conditions	Cd	Clf	Clr
Standard car	0.408	0.311	0.039
Move front bumper forward 1 in.	0.407	0.300	0.044
Lift rear edge of bonnet 1 in.	0.411	0.306	0.040
Return bumper/bonnet to standard			
Modify to ducted radiator	0.406	0.300	0.044
Lower front belly pan 1 in.	0.398	0.279	0.047
Blank off brake cooling ducts	0.404	0.297	0.045
Add new brake ducts below pan	0.399	0.263	0.053
Tape over A-pillar joints	0.397	0.265	0.057
Remove tape, remove door mirrors	0.387	0.261	0.051
Substitute low-drag mirrors	0.393	0.253	0.052
Fit flush headlamps	0.393	0.248	0.056
Blank off bonnet intake	0.389	0.240	0.059
Seal rear bonnet edge	0.387	0.233	0.064
Lower belly pan further 1 in.	0.385	0.206	0.066
Raise rear spoiler 1 in.	0.390	0.208	0.035
Tape over front tailgate edge	0.391	0.209	0.034
Raise front tailgate edge 0.5 in.	0.391	0.208	0.029
Fit deeper front air dam	0.367	0.139	0.048

LEFT *The first production Group A saloon to generate downforce in standard form is the Ford RS Cosworth, capable of over 150 mph in road going tune and destined to dominate circuit racing in the 1986 season*

AERODYNAMIC DEVELOPMENT OF RACING COUPÉ

Conditions	C_d	C_{lf}	C_{lr}
Standard car	0.356	0.245	0.070
Fit deeper front spoiler	0.351	0.209	0.087
Fit larger rear spoiler	0.345	0.222	−0.073
Racing trim, with ducted radiator, lowered fuel tank, vented inner wing panels, ride lowered 0.5 in.	0.362	0.231	0.055
Door mirrors removed	0.356	0.233	0.059
Modified brake cooling ducts	0.359	0.223	0.064
Remove radiator duct, restore standard brake ducts, seal vents	0.359	0.245	0.058
Raise lowered fuel tank 3 in.	0.357	0.241	0.056
Open 2 × 3 in. inner wing vents	0.359	0.240	0.056
Restore radiator duct	0.355	0.230	0.058
Add undertray to X-member	0.353	0.192	0.061
Blank off front grille	0.343	0.161	0.071
Tape up headlamps	0.342	0.151	0.075
Tape up bonnet, raise tailgate 1 in.	0.335	0.146	0.056
Restore tailgate, raise rear 1 in.	0.339	0.133	0.074
Seal heater intake, add rear wiper	0.337	0.126	0.079
Increase front spoiler depth 1 in.	0.335	0.127	0.085

BELOW *The MG Metro 6R4 Group B rally car uses aerodynamics primarily to generate downforce and provide engine cooling. Front and rear spoilers are well clear of the body surfaces and fully adjustable to suit different events*

The Audi Quattro Group B rally car depends on high engine power combined with four-wheel drive for its performance success. A basic front-end weight bias from the engine position eliminates the need for a front air dam

To put physical units on to the dimensionless coefficients quoted in these tables, it can be computed that the 0.311 front lift coefficient of the racing saloon, for example, is equivalent at 100 mph to about 170 lb positive lift at the front axle (enough to raise the ride height by 1.5 in.), while the 0.044 rear lift coefficient of the coupé equates to only about 25 lb positive lift.

As in the case of the racing prototypes described earlier in this chapter, reducing front end lift always increases rear lift and *vice-versa* due to the fulcrum effect of the lift couples about the car's pressure centre. Achieving low drag with minimum lift is a delicate fine-tuning process with close interrelated links between actions taken at the front end and the rear, which must always be investigated together and harmonized for the best overall effects.

American stock car racing

This category of saloon car racing (as it would be called in Europe) has very free controls on bodywork modifications. The objective is to provide high-speed spectator thrills. These unique cars, which bear only a passing resemblance to the models the American public can buy, are stripped out, welded up, lowered and stretched, as well as mechanically highly modified to reach lap speeds well up in the 200 mph bracket. Nonetheless, when aerodynamics became a new industry science, it was naturally applied to this racing category with some interesting results.

In 1969 the Chrysler Corporation were active participants in this sector of the sport with full factory support for entrants and a wide range of special products available. Their design team turned to aerodynamics as an alternative to continuing the established horsepower race for faster lap times. For very little development cost and without the need for extensive test programmes, they totally revised the aerodynamic characteristics of the Dodge Charger stock car, working on the simple premise that a 15 per cent reduction in body drag was worth at least an 85 bhp power increase.

The approach was to develop a three-eighths scale model for testing in both the Lockheed Georgia and the Wichita State University tunnels, followed by limited correlations on a full-size prototype. An unusual feature of this model was its detailed reproduction of the underfloor components and panel form, complete with fully functional model cooling fan and radiator system, driven by a miniature electric motor. Special attention was paid to ground effects by the installation of a ground plane detached from the tunnel floor.

In developing the aerodynamic performance, the limitations and constraints imposed by different stock car racing groups had to be considered. NASCAR (North American Stock Car Association for Racing), for example, limits ground clearance under the body to 6.5 in., under the oil sump to 5 in. and under the exhaust system to 4 in., although most organizations allow the fitting of non-standard front and rear spoilers.

Another major consideration was the dynamic qualities of the car at high speed as sensed by the driver. The technique for racing cars of this type on high speed banked tracks is specialized and derived from a tradition of 'midget' racing on short distance oval circuits, where most of the drivers involved gained their experience. They therefore prefer a car to develop aerodynamic oversteer in yaw by generating high sideforces at the front axle in a turn. The pressure centre is therefore arranged ahead of the centre of gravity, not behind as it would be for maximum straight line stability. Unlike the racing cars already discussed, stock car design also provides more downforce on the front axle than at the rear, to improve the high speed steering feel in a fundamentally unstable layout.

The development of the improved car, known as the Charger Daytona, followed the expected pattern of starting with an optimized front end and working back through each body detail in turn. Various low drag nose extensions were tried in the wind tunnel to improve penetration and induce low pressure under the car for optimum downforce. Although a 9 in. nose extension without a spoiler was found to reduce drag more than an 18 in. nose extension without one, when a 51 in. span by 5 in. chord spoiler was mounted 13 in. back from the nose at an angle of 45 degrees to the ground, the relative merits were reversed.

Spoiler effectiveness as a function of yaw angle was found to be very sensitive to front end shape. Although the addition of the spoiler on the new extended front end proved 4.5 times more effective at reducing drag than the addition of a similar spoiler to the previous short-nose design at zero yaw (straight ahead), both spoilers became totally ineffective at about 9 to 10 degrees of yaw. This confirms what might seem obvious after a little consideration of the basic concept, that spoilers are mostly forward acting devices. The less obvious result of the tests perhaps was the low angle of yaw at which they lost their effectiveness.

Vehicle attitude also had a significant effect on body drag, and on front end lift. While both body shapes were very sensitive to the angle of attack, the low drag long-nosed version required less nose-down attitude than the more bluff fronted earlier design. Optimum settings for the two cars were −0.5 and −1.5 degrees respectively. With the low drag car a steeper angle allowed front end lift to become downforce only for an unacceptable drag penalty.

The effects of the rear airfoil were also extremely interesting as it was mounted between twin vertical fins almost 24 in. above the rear deck, well clear of the normal surface boundary layer. It had a 58 in. span and a 7.5 in. chord. At an incidence angle of −10 degrees there was a drag penalty of 7 per cent combined with about −0.24 rear lift coefficient, compared with zero for no airfoil at all and −0.10 for a

Ford's Group B rally contender, the RS200, also uses four-wheel drive, but in a mid-engined layout. The eight-lamp arrangement destroys the air flow over the nose, proving the insignificance of low drag for an international rally car

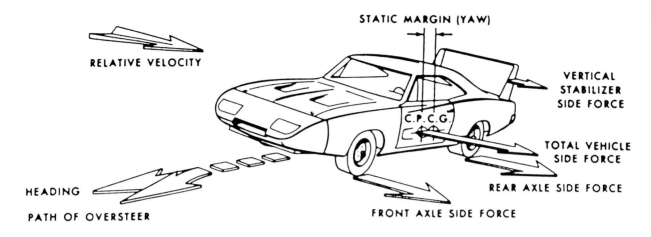

RELATIVE VELOCITY

STATIC MARGIN (YAW)

VERTICAL STABILIZER SIDE FORCE

C.P.C.G.

TOTAL VEHICLE SIDE FORCE

REAR AXLE SIDE FORCE

HEADING

PATH OF OVERSTEER

FRONT AXLE SIDE FORCE

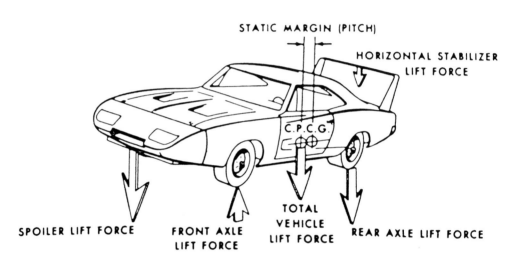

STATIC MARGIN (PITCH)

HORIZONTAL STABILIZER LIFT FORCE

C.P.C.G.

SPOILER LIFT FORCE

FRONT AXLE LIFT FORCE

TOTAL VEHICLE LIFT FORCE

REAR AXLE LIFT FORCE

For NASCAR racing, Chrysler developed their Dodge Charger Daytona in the Lockheed wind tunnel to generate aerodynamic oversteer by positioning the centre of pressure ahead of the centre of gravity. The nose spoiler became ineffective at 9–10 degrees of yaw

zero incidence angle. As in other cases, the front end lift increased as rear lift decreased due to the fulcrum effect of the airfoil position behind the rear axle centre line.

The results of all the Dodge developments led to a 5 mph increase in lap times and a new official lap record at one circuit very close to 200 mph. The aerodynamic knowledge gained through racing improved the state of the art understanding of aerodynamic effects in the most significant areas of handling at high speed, sidewind stability and the development of ultimate low drag features. The practicalities of providing adequate ground clearance to negotiate ramps and clear kerbs, combined with the need to provide sufficient engine cooling for all climates, and heater and ventilation intakes that can cope with tropical summers as well as arctic winters, all preclude the direct transfer of racing advances very far into the field of production cars for general sale.

12 Future trends

There are just three basic questions to be answered on how the science of aerodynamics is likely to develop in the next few years ahead. They involve a substantiated prediction of how much lower the threshold of drag reduction can be pushed, to be worthwhile, to be economic in design and manufacturing terms, and to be commercially acceptable to the majority of the car buying public. To deal with these points there are some technical facts to be discussed, some evidence to be quoted and some guesses to be made.

Associated with drag reduction are influences and side effects which seem increasingly likely to become major issues in the future. How will stability be maintained as Cd values get lower? Where will the *dynamics* of low drag transport cross over to exceed the *aerodynamics* in order of importance? Can the two be harmonized? And at the end of the day, how will the conflicting requirements of packaging people and meeting construction and use regulations be resolved? What compromises will have to be made, and where will the ultimate limit be set before aerodynamics starts to decline in importance?

Most of the clues to predicting the future can be found in today's trends, especially when they are assessed against yesterday's yardsticks and projected ahead. To indicate what the leading designers are planning for the end of this decade (and into the next), four special cars will be analyzed in depth. Three of them concentrate on the lower end of the market, where maximum sales are achieved and the direction towards which there is a pronounced market swing. One (the Ford Probe V) demonstrates the extremes needed to make any further radical progress from the 0.25–0.30 Cd limit set by today's production methods. It does not function as a working prototype yet, but its purpose is clearly just as valid as all the concept studies before it. Its achievement is in performing as a styling model with a better Cd than a jet-powered aircraft. Its production realization (although a running prototype is being built during 1986) must wait for more progress in design and materials.

Volkswagen Student and the BL ECV3

Even more aerodynamically impressive perhaps, and rumoured to be nearly ready for a production launch, is the Volkswagen research vehicle called the Student. This manages to combine a basic droplet shape with a totally replanned interior package in a way that many observers have found aesthetically more pleasing to the eye than all other low-drag shapes before it. As a solid indicator of what the future has to hold, it sets new aerodynamic standards.

LEFT *Volkswagen's little Student is a leading example of how cars at the smallest end of the market are likely to look in the early 1990s. It combines a low drag shape with pleasant looks and a practical interior package*

The roots of this minimum size four-seater saloon actually go back as far as 1975, when Volkswagen Research investigated the effects of downsizing the smallest car in their model line-up. Working on a Polo interior package, they shortened the exterior length from 143.7 in. to only 130 in., without losing any significant interior room. A running prototype called 'Chicco' was built to demonstrate the concept of a sub-Polo saloon, but never developed for production.

From this baseline another research prototype called 'Student' was designed and built in 1982. It extended the philosophy of the Chicco a stage further by retaining the Polo front seat package inside, but shortchanging the occasionally used rear seat dimensions, reducing the overall length further to only 123.2 in. (the size of the original 1959 Mini). More significant in every way was the drag coefficient of only 0.31 achieved for this car.

Just after the French government research efforts first went on view at the Paris Motor Show in September 1982, BL Technology Ltd revealed their ideas of how the car of the future would make better use of the fuel it burned. Their research project was called ECV3 (Energy Conservation Vehicle No 3) and combined a low drag, space-efficient body with low weight and a very advanced engine. It consolidated earlier work (on ECV1 and ECV2, which were low drag developments based on pre-production Metro prototypes) in a new and larger concept that would exceed 100 mph, accelerate from 0 to 60 mph in under 12 seconds and return better than 60 mpg in everyday driving.

To improve the consumption of typical cars in the same size class by 75 per cent was a bold ambition based on a lot of background experience in materials and systems. During the preliminary aerodynamic work a number of lessons emerged,

ABOVE RIGHT *BL Technology developed this original five-door family car, called ECV-3, to demonstrate many advanced features, including weight savings, new materials and a very low drag coefficient of only 0.24 with the cooling intake closed*

BELOW RIGHT *At the rear, ECV-3 used a novel wing arrangement designed to move the centre of pressure rearwards for improved stability. As drag values are reduced, these kinds of aerodynamic aids are going to become essential*

however. No matter how carefully the upper surfaces were shaped, it was virtually impossible to reach drag coefficient values below 0.33 with a conventional lower surface to the pressed steel floorpan. The ultimate limit, which probably lies around 0.30, was verified by other low drag cars in production and design research efforts like the Ford Probe III (see Chapter 9).

Detachable undertrays, in BL's view, were rejected on the grounds that they intruded on precious ground clearance, added weight, cost more and made servicing more difficult. So they followed the UNI-CAR lead by redesigning the floorpan from a smooth undersurface, continuous from front to rear as far as possible, unbroken by cross-members and suspension attachment points and devoid of major variations in the flow area between the sheet metal and the road. If this could be achieved, it was argued, there would be less of a drag penalty by encouraging free flow than in adding a front air dam to divert the air in other directions.

Various upper body shapes were tried around the dimensional hard points dictated by the very practical packaging targets, which precluded the ultra-low, sleek shape selected for most other futuristic exercises. In the early stages Cd values as low as 0.22 were recorded on four different quarter-scale models of both the fastback profile eventually chosen and a squarebacked estate car with strongly tapered planform. But the full-size models built later were measured at 0.25 (0.24 with the automatic cooling air intake closed), a remarkable achievement in a car measuring only 152 in. from bumper to bumper.

As well as the smooth underbody mentioned above, the design which evolved during wind tunnel development included a very distinctive and detached rear wing. Its purpose was both to reduce the wake area behind the car and to move the centre of pressure rearwards, to improve stability which tends to deteriorate as drag coefficients get lower. A different solution to the same kind of problem was developed in the shape of a small dorsal fin for Ford's Probe V described later in this chapter.

The breakdown of fuel economy reductions achieved with ECV3 reveals the limits likely to be reached in future low drag cars. About 40 per cent of the gains made were from powertrain improvements (increased engine efficiency matched to higher overall gearing) and about 37 per cent from a 33 per cent weight reduction. Some 5 per cent was saved by attention to rolling resistance and 18 per cent from aerodynamics.

Developed as Project 2002 but exhibited at motor shows as ELTECH, Ford of Europe's research vehicle was meant to show how tomorrow's car might look and function in the late 1990s. Its drag coefficient was 0.31, which is generally reckoned to be an economic limit for a small family car

Ford's Project 2002 and the ultimate Probe V

By the time it was ready for public showing at the 1985 Frankfurt Motor Show, Ford's European research vehicle (initially known as Project 2002 to relate to the year in which its engineering and appearance might be commonplace) was much closer than 17 years to realization. So its name was changed to ELTECH (a contraction of electronic technology) to reflect the many features and details incorporated in the total design. Under the control of a practical engineering research team, rather than a group of aerodynamic stylists, its production feasibility was strictly 'tomorrow' rather than 'the year after next'. That fact constrained the achievements attempted in the field of low drag and reflected a perceptible swing away from the aerodynamic minefield where, it can be convincingly argued, the last few percentage point gains have little relevance in today's driving environment. As BL Technology had clearly shown, improvements

in engine efficiency at this stage have more than twice the potential value of further drag reductions.

The essence of ELTECH (Project 2002) therefore lies in its powertrain efficiency, dramatically enhanced by computer-controlled systems and some clever in-novation. There are some aerodynamic gains, of course, but only as far as was needed to reduce the Cd from the 0.36 value achieved on the 1986 Escort to a level of 0.31.

Significantly in many ways, ELTECH shows the way design emphasis is moving back from the 0.30 threshold as fuel prices fall in real economic terms. Of course the car makes some worthwhile progress, with a new design of shallow-height headlamp, for example, that will bring nose section radii down for better air penetration in the next few years. The clever integration of the moulded rear bumper into the start of an enclosed wheelcover is a trend which is bound to be picked up and extended into other concept cars and eventually production models. But the statement ELTECH makes most strongly is that all the 'teardrops' and all the 'bubbles' in the world, efficient as they are, are not yet commercially viable in the volume car market where traditional styling values and a desire for comforting familiarity are more important than the price of fuel.

Probe V was designed in the Ford US studios for a totally different purpose. First revealed in public at the 1985 Tokyo Motor Show, it represented the most extreme and extraordinary thoughts of a young and adventurous team whose task was 'to design and engineer a car with the shape and technologies anticipated in the (long-term) future'. Its objective was to demonstrate as much as to anticipate, so that Ford management could tune in to concepts ten years ahead, get comfortable with the new shapes being planned and sound out public opinion on the direction of

things to come. It might even (in the words of Don Kopka, vice president in charge of design at Ford) 'educate and condition potential customers'.

In outline the shape of Probe V reverts to the idealized teardrop which has been fundamental to low vehicle drag since the very beginning of aerodynamic science. It has no protrusions at all on the exterior surface, and none on the underbody either. The wheel cutouts are fully covered, using the same kind of flexible polyurethane membrane concept as Probe IV at the front, and the whole of the upper surface above the waistline is fabricated in glass. And, like the MG EX-E which appeared at almost exactly the same time, it is very significantly totally devoid of spoilers.

Probe V managed as a full-size (but non-running) prototype to record a Cd value of only 0.137 in the Lockheed-Georgia wind tunnel, comfortably the lowest figure ever seen on a car supposedly able to accept fully representative mechanical components. The cooling intakes for its centrally-mounted transverse turbocharged engine were closed, as they might be perhaps at the legal US speed limit of 55 mph which, it is claimed by Ford, takes only 6 bhp to be maintained. Under more typical European conditions of 70 mph, Probe V still requires less than 10 bhp to propel it, provided its low drag is actually achieved when the running prototypes are completed in 1986.

An integral part of the research project is to investigate the interaction between very low drag, handling and sidewind stability. So a small dorsal fin was added to the centre of the rear decklid, moulded in glass to reduce its visual impact and of such small surface dimensions that its effects could hardly be significant in aerodynamic terms. But as drag gets lower and the aerodynamic centre of pressure moves forward, stability aids like fins are going to become important. The one on Probe V is to test public reaction to what might otherwise be interpreted as just a styling revival.

Other elements essential to Probe V's achievements are its shallow front headlamps stretching round most of the well radiused nose, a 69-degree windscreen rake angle and its heavily cambered rear end planform. As on Probe IV, the engine cooling outlet is used to generate positive pressure in the wake area behind the car, as a means of using waste energy usefully. Its greatest shortcoming in practical terms is the low overall height of only 47 in. which demanded doors cut into the roof nearly as far as the centreline of the car, and an intricate sliding mechanism to open them adequately for easy access in confined parking places.

Efficiency in perspective

Judged in isolation, drag coefficient levels appear to have settled at just over the 0.30 value for cars above the market mid-point, and around 0.35 for cars any smaller. The longer a car becomes the easier it is to achieve low drag without resorting to the expensive underbody shrouding required for more development progress. The table below shows the results of applying a simple relationship between length and Cd on a variety of modern shapes and highlights some of the real achievements and some of the less advanced results.

Ford's Probe V, which has a Cd of well below 0.20, uses a small dorsal fin to maintain stability in a basically undisturbed airstream. Although it was built as a show car at the end of 1985, it later became a full running prototype

DRAG COEFFICIENT VERSUS LENGTH FOR AERODYNAMIC DESIGNS

Model	Length	Cd	Length × Cd
1981 VW Auto 2000	158.1 in.	0.25	39.5
1981 UNI-CAR	176.9 in.	0.23	40.7
1982 Ford Sierra	173.0 in.	0.34	58.8
1982 Audi 100	189.0 in.	0.30	56.7
1982 Peugeot VERA PLUS	165.0 in.	0.31	51.2
1982 Volkswagen Student	123.2 in.	0.31	38.2
1982 Renault VESTA	126.0 in.	0.25	31.5
1982 BL ECV3	152.0 in.	0.24	36.5
1984 Renault 25	182.1 in.	0.28	51.0
1984 Citroen ECO 2000	137.6 in.	0.31	42.7
1984 Vauxhall Astra GTE	157.4 in.	0.30	47.2
1985 Ford ELTECH	156.3 in.	0.31	48.4
1985 Ford Probe V	191.6 in.	0.14	26.8

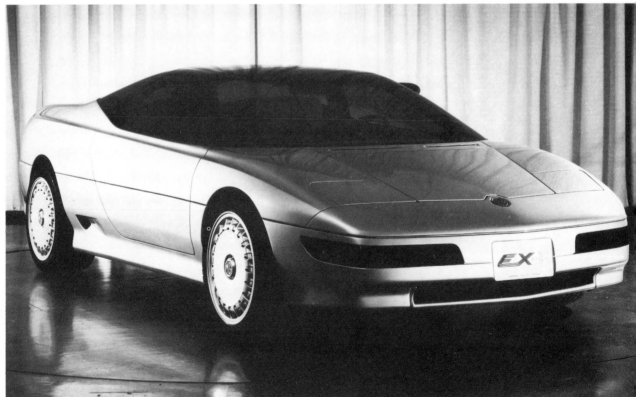

ABOVE *Across the Atlantic
General Motors' designers
regularly wheel out their
thoughts on futuristic design.
Their Aero 2000 shown here
was later developed into the
Aero 2002 with a Cd of only
0.14*

LEFT, ABOVE AND BELOW *The
MG EX-E, which appeared
unexpectedly at the 1985
Frankfurt Motor Show, uses
a clean body with no visible
spoilers to lead design trends
towards the next century.
Under its smooth skin the
advanced four-wheel drive
components of the 6R4 rally
car had been cleverly
shoehorned*

Ironically in the application of aerodynamic principles, it is another totally different stimulus that will most likely bring about the breakthrough required. New European noise regulations, applicable to new cars in a series of changes over the next two years, require the sound generated by a car driving past a microphone in a specifically defined test to be halved. In many cases that will mean cutting engine noise by as much as 90 per cent, which could lead to sound encapsulation of the engine bay with an acoustic front belly pan. And if that comes about, the aerodynamicists will immediately be able to cut drag by another valuable step.

Most vehicle legislation, however, conflicts with efficiency improvements, instead of providing the means to achieve more progress. Front towing eyes, for example, must somehow be positioned to protrude from the surface of an air dam and a vertical housing for the front licence plate must be integrated into a nose section already constrained by fixed bumper heights and an optimized cooling air intake. Door mirrors, as mentioned earlier, must still provide a safety knock-back feature, precluding aerodynamic fairings until the regulations are changed. There are also standards on fields of view, windscreen wiped areas and double-image refraction which restrict both maximum windscreen angle and the surface geometry of the rear end.

Functional constraints are almost as much of a design challenge, with underbody clearance for 30 degree ramp angles required front and rear, provision for snow chain fitment restricting wheelcover installations and head-to-header rail proximity inside the cabin being a necessary safety prerequisite. And it will be a long time before most manufacturers feel the cost of flush-mounted drop-down door windows justifies the benefits to be gained in aerodynamic terms.

So in realistic terms, unless there are further unpredictable disruptions of oil supplies, the aerodynamic design of production cars has reached a viable limit on a plateau at a Cd value of around 0.30. Although the technology exists to lower this further to about 0.25, progress in fuel economy (which has been the strongest development motivation over the past decade) is much more likely to swing towards power units where environmental pressure for clean air is forcing massive investments in new designs and new manufacturing facilities.

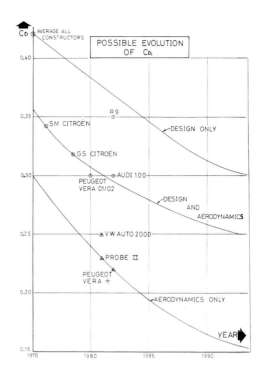

Volkswagen research, like that of most other car makers at the leading edge of aerodynamic development, shows a distinct levelling off of drag reductions by 1990 with production cars likely to fall between Cd values of 0.26 and 0.34

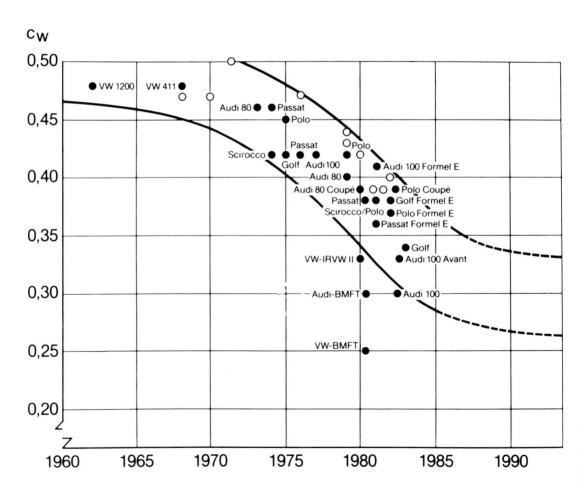

Index